MW01625955

Lessons From the Wilderness
Find Your Way Home and Finish Well

Manuscript Updated May 2022

Book	ISBN 978-1-7780641-0-4
EBook	ISBN 978-1-7780641-1-1
Audio	ISBN 978-1-7780641-2-8

LESSONS

FROM

THE

WILDERNESS

Find Your Way Home
and Finish Well

Bill Spangler

DEDICATION

To Gwen, Kristen, and Karin who
encouraged and stayed close as I journeyed

To the teachers of life lessons, who are doing
a great work when you do not even know the parts
you are playing in the story of others

To those who find themselves on a wilderness
journey right now, and are looking for a compass
to point the way

Response to *Lessons From the Wilderness*

This book brings hope to every hurting, broken soul. A must read for every heart that has experienced pain and disappointment. It offers deep spiritual insight and practical wisdom for healing, wholeness and "finishing well."

Fay Cherepuschak, Registered Nurse

Lessons From the Wilderness is packed with pithy, wisdom filled statements which opened new windows for me. How refreshing it is to realize that giving our best is, all by itself, actually good enough, and we can rest peacefully on that thought alone. I can see this book being used as a small group study resource, a window of freedom to burdened believers who are looking for a way out and up from negative inner voices, and a practical tool for pastors and teachers who want to be equipped to lead others (and self) out of the dark places of life.

J. A. Nash, Retired Pastor

As I read through Bill's wilderness journey, it felt like we were having a healing conversation. Bill shares gently and transparently, from his heart, in a way that allows the reader to relate. Through each phase of the journey he highlights the underlying source of his strength and redemption - God's forgiveness and acceptance. This book allowed me to pause at many points to consider how I might better navigate my own challenges and live in a space of acceptance and gratitude.

Lara Melashenko, Education Leader

Bill's understanding of guilt, shame, forgiveness, grace, and potential are truly insightful and profound. *Lessons From the Wilderness* not only sets out to restore the soul, but to redesign a life to realize its potential and legacy. Bill understands the human condition and points to Godly wisdom through lessons learned. The Life Lessons and Compass Points will keep you coming back to reread. From the insights and wisdom gained here, you will not be the same.

James Lalonde, Mental Health Consultant

For every account of fame or fortune, there are a thousand stories that remain unwritten, obscure, unspoken. Bill has chosen to write the story of his journey in a way that is compelling, and inspiring. C.S. Lewis once said: "God can take a lizard on your back and turn it into a steed on which you ride into the kingdom of heaven." From his personal journey, Bill has drawn principles that when upon personal reflection, and applied in every life, will guide us to be better people. People with regrets, moving toward self-acceptance. People journeying from shame to hope. People with a life lived with personal integrity and honor. Ultimately this is a story of the power of redemption.

Ken Crawford, Retired Pastor

In this book, *Lessons From the Wilderness*, Bill Spangler peels back the layers of pain and disappointment in his life and many others, then courageously blazes a trail of lessons that lead you and me like a compass guiding us out of the deep dark wilderness of life's anguish and disconnections.

Annette Stanwick, BScN, Speaker, Freedom Facilitator and Coach
Author of *Forgiveness: The Mystery and Miracle*

Resisting the human tendency to hide some innermost thoughts - Bill allows God to use his journey through the proverbial wilderness experience as a 'Christ-Object-Lesson' pathway of spiritual principles for redemption and restoration. *Lessons from the Wilderness* is cataract laser surgery for the disease of self-pity, isolation, and fear. A textbook for the downtrodden, despairing, and maligned.

Josiah Rambally Jr., Addictions Counselor/Missionary

My healing journey could be a book on its own! The shock and pain offered no easy options for moving forward. As we journeyed, applying the lessons spoken about in this book, we were able to rebuild our marriage relationship beyond what I could have imagined. Bill's vulnerability, strength and courage written in *Lessons From the Wilderness* demonstrates his commitment to finish well.

Gwen Spangler, Loving Wife, and "Wilderness Companion"

CONTENTS

I believe that the wilderness is where God is found.

Jonathan Kozol

Today, I am not the person I was when I entered the wilderness! I am wiser, stronger, and now carry a backpack full of experience that is searching for a place of expression.

From the Wilderness

Moses spent forty years in the wilderness and still fulfilled his destiny.

By Faith Medi

INTRODUCTION

There are many people that I would personally consider to be heroes, and Moses is one of them. Of all my heroes, he is the inspiration that makes this book a reality. Here's why. Moses and I have a lot in common.

If you've heard of Moses, but don't really know much about him, let me give you a short version of his story, as it is told in the Bible. He was born about 3,400 years ago in the land of Egypt. Moses was born to a Hebrew mother and father, who were slaves, at a time when the very nervous king of Egypt made a decree that all baby boys born to Hebrew women were to be put to death at birth.

King Pharaoh ruled with a heavy hand and had the Hebrew people as slaves under his fist. The thought of a leader being born to alter his grip on his people and the slaves he controlled was not a thought he wanted to entertain, so his decree was meant to make sure that would never happen.

When Moses was born, his mother, knowing his life was at risk, hid him in a basket in the reeds in the river where he was watched over by his older sister, Miriam. Pharaoh's daughter came to the river to bathe and noticed the basket. Upon seeing the baby, she instantly put the story together in her mind and promptly "adopted" the baby for her own; no paperwork required! Miriam offered to find someone to nurse the baby, and immediately ran to get her mother, who, of course, was also the baby's mother.

The Egyptian Princess gave assurance to Moses' mother of his safety from the death decree. The plan was made that she would come to get Moses when he was older to take him to the palace to live with her. Moses' mother now knew that she had just a short time to instill in him the values and beliefs that she and his father lived by, values that she believed were from God Himself.

As previously arranged, in due time, Moses went to the palace to live with his adoptive Egyptian Princess mother. While his biological mother prayed he would never forget his roots and heritage, Moses also learned all the secrets and tools of leadership and war that the ranking officials of Egypt saw fit to teach him.

At around forty years of age, Moses committed the crime of murder. He saw an Egyptian man viciously beating one of the Hebrew slaves and took matters into his own hands. He quickly buried the body in the sand and left the scene.

The very next day he saw two Hebrew men quarrelling. He pleaded with them to stop, to which one replied, "Do you plan to kill me as you killed that Egyptian yesterday?" Exodus 2:14 (NLT)

Moses realized that his secret was not a secret and that his life was now in danger. When Pharoah heard about it, he wanted Moses arrested and executed. Moses left Egypt immediately and after a long journey, found refuge many miles away with a man who lived with his family in the desert area of Midian. His host was rich in flocks and herds. Moses accepted the invitation to stay with them. He fell in love with one of the man's daughters, got married and settled into a new lifestyle far away from the palace and from his people. He became a shepherd and cared for sheep in the wilderness for the next 40 years.

The desert is a quiet place, and Moses no doubt endured many lonely days. I wonder how often his mind went to Egypt and his Hebrew background. I can easily believe that he often berated himself with the question, "How did I end up here?"

The story goes on to say that one day, the God of Heaven personally spoke to Moses to reveal the calling on his life. God wanted him to go back to Egypt now and lead the Hebrew people out of slavery to a new land that God had in mind for them.

Moses was absolutely sure that God had the wrong person and that He must be looking for someone else. Alternatively, God was adamant that He had made no mistake, and that Moses was indeed the man He was looking for.

Moses came up with several reasons why he could or should not accept this request, and the story says that God got angry at Moses' excuses. I like to think that whatever that anger looked like, God was also saying to Himself, "This is not the Moses who left Egypt. Now, here's a man I can work with!"

Forty years earlier, Moses had been sure of himself and a "take charge" kind of man. If murder was necessary, then it was acceptable.

He no doubt could rationalize the obvious choice of himself as a leader; after all, look at his experience and resume. A Hebrew, intimately knowledgeable about the life of his people, and a man intimately knowledgeable about the government of Egypt. Perfect!!

Now, after 40 years in the wilderness, things were very different. Moses was a man who was unsure of himself, and he was timid. The haughty man was now humble; the arrogant man was now afraid.

What made the difference? What did Moses think about during those forty long years? What were the lessons that Moses received and learned during the time in the wilderness? What had moved him from mighty to meek?

The short story from there is that Moses reluctantly went back to Egypt, stood in front of Pharaoh and spoke as a voice for God, asking that God's people be released from slavery. Pharaoh refused, but after a series of devastating supernatural plagues on the nation, Pharaoh relented, and Moses led his Hebrew people out of slavery into freedom. He was their leader for another 40 years before he died. He was mighty and is referred to constantly in the history of the Hebrew/Jewish people to this very day.

Here's why this story makes Moses a hero to me.

Every life has high and low times. Pleasant times and dry times, happy times and hard times, as well as quiet times and what one might categorize as "non-productive" years. Mine is no different.

My experience is a bit like that of Moses. I was invited by God to be a leader. I was a pastor, and for a time I was a leader of pastors. I felt loved, accepted, and lived a life of joy and fulfillment. I was living the dream of the things that mattered to me and that which I valued.

However, like Moses, I too made a critical error. There was a period of time when I was living a double life. I made the choice to be involved in a relationship outside of my marriage. My poor decisions and choices hurt many, many people. I broke a promise to God and disappointed Him. I brought shame to myself and pain to my wife, daughters, parents and siblings. My choices created pain and dishonour for another person and negatively impacted her family. I destroyed the trust of countless people who worked with me, trusted me, knew me, or knew of me. I placed a dark shadow on the integrity of pastoral ministry and brought sadness and grief to God and to His angels. I undermined my own integrity. I had no choice but to pack the tools of the ministry I loved into boxes, stuff them under the stairs in my house, and wonder if they would ever be of value or use to me again.

I have experienced my own personal wilderness journey, and I have often thought about Moses and the lessons that transformed him into the man he became. He had many long days to reflect on the path of his life, as have I. In my reflection, I have considered several events, learning experiences, books I have read, or even just simple teachings and phrases that have impacted me. In some way, each one has positively influenced my thinking and shaped me into who I am today. These lessons are as valuable to me as gold. They have given me strength, purpose, and direction. They have picked me up when I am down and allowed me to move forward when it would have been easier to quit. They have given me direction when I was unable to read my moral compass clearly. And, they are too good to keep for myself.

These thoughts, lessons and truths are not secrets, and they are not mine. I do not own them or claim them. I have learned them from others. I cherish them because they have caused me to grow, stretch and learn. They are the wisdom of life, and each of us puts our own personal stamp of expression on them.

I want to share them with you, in my words, from my journey through my wilderness.

This book is not an account of my failure and my mistakes. There will be no details of that story spelled out here. I want to focus on the lessons I learned from that time in my life, and I only say the little bit that I have in order to give a brief insight to the context of where my wilderness lessons began.

I entered my personal wilderness on April 20, 2000, the evening I spoke with my wife, Gwen, and told her the truth of my secret. For the first time, she became aware of the double life I had been living. From there I began the process of resignation from the ministry I loved, and entered the journey of healing and rebuilding my life.

Today, I am not the person I was when I entered the wilderness! I am wiser, stronger, and now carry a backpack full of experience that is searching for a place of expression. I trust that something in these pages, even one thing, will impact you in a way that will be worth underlining and remembering for use in the days of your journey.

Moses is my hero because we have so much in common. Life was good for Moses until he made that fatal decision. Life was also good for me, until, like Moses, I too made a decision of fatal error.

Like Moses, my secret had been exposed.

Like Moses, I knew that life was about to drastically change, but I did not know where it would take me.

Like Moses, the future was very uncertain and very dark.

I can only assume, but I believe Moses must have asked himself, "How did I get here? How could I have been so foolish?" I too have asked myself that question many, many times.

Like Moses, I suddenly found myself in a wilderness of time and space that was now all my own. It was different from anything I had ever experienced before. I was stumbling along alone, scanning my compass and searching for direction, anchor points, and a place of peace.

But, also like Moses, the lessons learned in the wilderness have prepared me for days of opportunity and purpose.

And, like Moses, God never lost sight of me. He knew where I was at all times. He gave me reason to believe that despite the dishonorable decisions I made and the opportunities I lost, He still had an interest in me and reasons to stay close. He just needed to take me to His school for a time.

Lessons From the Wilderness is an insight into my journey through dark times, to years of renewed joy, and peace. I have discovered that however dark the road one travels, and the various struggles one may experience, there is always the opportunity to finish well.

In a way, it's a small picture of God's plan of salvation for all mankind. He had plans for us, but humanity rebelled and went into a wilderness. Life as we know it, with all of its challenges was never God's original design. He desires to restore us, and we are blessed by Him and His presence with us through it all.

The chapters in this book sometimes repeat details, facts, or stories. I have chosen to do so on purpose to give context or the timing of a new or particular lesson I am sharing from the same event or story. The book is not designed to progress in any specific order. I am not attempting a chronological glimpse of my life, just a few snapshots along the way. Reading a chapter because a title spontaneously catches your attention will not in any way interrupt the flow of reading all the chapters in order.

Some of the lessons I will share in this book are directly connected to the poor decisions and consequences in my life I have just referred to that took me on this wilderness journey. Other lessons were learned from many personal growth experiences I have been privileged to experience along the way. Each one has had an impact for change in my life. It is the fact that I was on this journey in the first place that opened up these opportunities for learning. I share them with you, hoping that at least one of them can impact your life as well.

At the end of each chapter, I have summarized some of the lessons I learned along the way. Then, I have also added some "Compass Points" to contemplate. These are in the form of questions where the answers might possibly point you in a direction that will help you to better navigate life.

Grab a backpack. Come journey with me and see if there are some lessons you might want to toss in there and hang on to for further reference. Maybe something I learned will be the perfect reference point to help you find what you are looking for.

PLEASE NOTE

I have chosen not to reference any personal names in the stories I have shared. While each one deserves recognition for the impact they have made on my life, there are many more whom I have not mentioned, and I could not name them all.

I want the learning points from my journey to be the emphasis of this book and that is the primary purpose of writing it. While the people in my journey are precious to me for the parts they played, I chose not to have the reader be distracted in any way by the recognition of the names of the individuals involved. You may find yourself here as you read, or you may personally know one or many of the people I have referenced in my journey. Rather than have a name take you down a path of memories of your own about that person I thought it best to keep the focus on the lesson itself, not the teacher of the lesson.

INTRODUCTION

NOTES FOR MY BACKPACK

The major problem of life is learning how to handle the costly interruptions. The door that slams shut, the plan that got sidetracked, the marriage that failed. Or that lovely poem that didn't get written because someone knocked on the door.

Martin Luther King Jr.

First, let me finish. Then interrupt.

Brian Spellman

We must stop regarding unpleasant or unexpected things as interruptions of real life. The truth is that interruptions are real life.

C.S. Lewis

1

THE GIFT OF INTERRUPTION

In April of 2000, I found my world incredibly interrupted. It was a result of my own choices and actions, but nevertheless it was completely turned upside down. It was as abrupt as hitting a solid rock wall on the side of a mountain. There was no flexibility or give whatsoever, and everything about life as I had known it was changed forever. My reputation was in shambles. My relationship with my wife and family was ripped wide open. My future ability to financially provide for myself and my family was completely up in the air and unknown.

I had a choice to make. I could live in the world of victimhood and cry, "Poor me." I could lash out and attempt to sidestep the truth. I could look for ways to lay blame. Or I could take a deep breath, plant my feet firmly on the ground and see what I could do when the sun rose again in the morning. In all honesty, it took several sunrises to sort out the chaos in my head and start thinking clearly, but that was my ultimate goal right from the start.

Who likes being interrupted? Kids sure don't! The audacity of a parent to come along just when the fun is reaching its best energy and announce that it's bedtime!! Or, just in the middle of a good story book, dad takes a phone call that is urgent, and the story is left hanging.

There is no stage in life that is free from or gets accustomed to interruptions. Sometimes kids have no choice but to deal with parents who have decided to end their relationship and suddenly the children have two separate homes to spend time in. Life as they knew it was interrupted, big time! All they ever wanted was the home they knew to stay intact.

Teenagers are forced to deal with broken hearts as that special someone they had romantic feelings for has decided that someone else is more charming than they are. The happy relationship world they were enjoying for the past weeks or months is suddenly turned upside down.

Adult life has the potential to be changed in a moment, for a variety of reasons. A car breakdown or a crash. A report from the doctor. A break-up or the request for a divorce. The death of a family member or best friend. A child who makes a not-so-wise decision that suddenly involves the police. An unexpected job change. These are all rather major.

Gwen and I were driving along one sunny day on an open, major, four-lane highway. I saw what I thought was a paper bag on the road ahead, and, since traffic was busy, I just decided to drive over it. About two seconds before impact, I realized it was, in fact, not a bag but a rock about the size of a basketball that had fallen off a truck. That "little" rock put my vehicle out of commission for about four months and caused several thousand dollars of damage. In two seconds, life changed dramatically. Thankfully, we were not hurt but it was a serious interruption to the big picture of our lives.

There are simple or happy interruptions, too. A ringing phone in the middle of watching something on television, or right at that intense moment in the book you are enjoying. A child who requires immediate attention while you are finishing that project that needs only fifteen more minutes to complete. A red light when you are in a hurry and every second counts. Suddenly finding out that just when you were done having children, you will in fact have one more. Or even the happiness of having a child for the first time can really put life on a different trajectory. The examples are varied and endless.

We have all been there at some time or other. Life was maybe not everything you were hoping it would be, but it was manageable and moving along with steady prediction, when suddenly, it wasn't any more. I have read my share of stories and biographies of people who have experienced major upheaval in their lives. When the page was turned to continue the story in the next chapter, life was totally changed for them. Often not in a good way. Much inspiration comes from watching people go through interruptions with class, dignity, and integrity.

What inspires us when watching and reading about the lives of other people, is seeing them go through the interruptions of life in a way that brings healing and direction. I think of people as world renowned as Corrie Ten Boom who walked out of a concentration camp and went on to travel the world, teaching about life interruptions and the value of forgiveness. She had been enjoying a fabulous little life on a simple street in Holland, providing a place of refuge for those who were oppressed by the war, and at the end of one fateful day, she and her family became prisoners of war. Her father and sister died as a result, yet she was able to move through all that grief, loss and unspeakable interruption of her life to a place of peace, commitment and life-purpose.

I also think of people as unknown as the mother and father whom I watched shovel dirt onto a tiny casket and then go home to do what it takes in order to make a life for the children who they still had to care for. Parents watch as adult children deal with separation and brokenness and are somewhat helpless except to stand by and be there for them and for their grandchildren. But the sun always rises the next morning. Moving on with life is a requirement that comes to all of us at some point along the way.

While all seem destined from time to time to face an interruption, the challenge is managed in very different ways. Some stand completely frozen in time from then on. I remember a woman telling me that her husband had died a year earlier in the process of rescuing their children from drowning. She went on to tell me, through her tears, that "Our children lost both parents that day. He died, and I have just sat and cried every day since. My kids don't have either parent right now." The struggle to see a new sunrise was intense, and she knew she needed to move on, but did not have a clue as to how to begin.

Others get angry and hate the event that caused the upheaval, as well as all the changes in life that come as a result of the interruption. They get angry at the person who caused the change. Some even get angry at a person who has died because life has changed so rapidly and drastically. They get angry with themselves for being angry. Everything and everyone seem to be an irritant and part of the overall problem. The eyes are blurred, and the emotions are raw because of the interruption that changed everything.

Some find it possible to take it in stride, and although the rhythm of life has changed, the purpose for life has not. They may stumble or even fall for a time, but that is not the end of the story by any means.

It's one chapter out of many. It's a time and place in the big picture that makes the rest of the story come alive.

One of the things that may help at a time of an interruption in life is to ask a very hard question. "What are the gifts that I can find from this interruption?"

You may go into minor shock from that question and incredulously wonder how I could even ask it. Fair enough, and I understand. However, it is still a valid question. Nothing happens in a vacuum. There are always other things that are changed and impacted along with the actual interruption itself. Often the effects of an interruption shift the rhythm of life for many people, even though the actual event focuses on only one person. Whole families and groups of friends can be impacted by the events in one person's life.

What I'm asking you to consider is what would happen if, once there is time to catch your breath after your interruption, you step back and ask, "In the midst of all this chaos, what are the gifts I can see coming out of it?"

Take the Covid-19 situation as an example. Everyone on the planet has been impacted by that one interruption. Whatever perspective you might be looking at it from, are there any gifts that can come from it all? I suggest that there are a few.

Families have slowed down and found out what it is like to spend more quality time together. Travel has been slowed down, and while that may not be a gift to the airline or hotel industry, individual people have found that staying home for a bit has brought amazing rest and healing from frenzied schedules that kept life out of balance.

Another gift that has come is that families have discovered and explored some of the points of interests and adventures that they had overlooked right in the neighborhood they live in. Often it is just accepted that the places to put on the "must see" list are many miles away. Many exciting discoveries were made right "next door" as a result of the travel interruption that was experienced.

For some, it's been a time for catching up on unaccomplished "to do" lists. For others, it's been a time to read and let the mind rest. For some spouses, it has provided an opportunity to become reacquainted after spending so much time running hectic schedules that went in opposite directions.

I understand that there were downsides to suddenly having everything turned upside down, but what happens when we focus on the gifts that come from it rather than all the things that are terrible?

There is truth in a statement that says, "How we do anything is how we do everything." In other words, if one is not able to find gifts, but only focus on the negative things about the Covid world, it is probably also true that they are not able to find any gifts about any experience in life that does not go as expected. If one only sees the downside in one situation, how often, upon reflection, is it discovered that they only see the downside of any situation. When that happens, life can get very heavy, dark, and cynical.

So, back to my own personal interruption. I found that one of the best ways to move forward was to start thinking about the gifts that I could count from this head-on-collision with life. I didn't think of it in those terms at the time, but upon reflection I am now able to list several. The pages of this book spell out many lessons learned in the days and years following that time, but I want to briefly summarize some gifts that emerged for me.

I was able to stop and recalibrate my personal honesty gauge which had been set aside and ignored while I was living a double life. To finally get back to what I knew to be a life of integrity and start afresh was a beautiful thing all by itself.

I loved my career, which was in fact a calling, not just a job. I was a pastor because I responded to an inner "knowing" that told me I had no choice. Being a pastor was what I was called to do. Now, when that was suddenly not an option anymore, I found it necessary to search out other ways to bring help and healing to broken people in a broken world. I knew I would always be a pastor at heart. I also knew I was not cut out to simply find a job somewhere that gave me a paycheck. My new vocation would also have to be fulfilling to my heart and soul as well. In due time I was able to find several options to earn a living while serving people. It has been energizing to my soul and I have enjoyed the journey of the discovery of it all. While at that time I had been trained in only one career path, I discovered that there is a big world of options to explore that I had not known about.

I received the incredible gift of finding out the depth of the friendships that I possessed. People who were willing to stand beside me, to be seen with me, to still call me friend even in my darkest moments, brought amazing healing to my wounded soul. I have kept letters from people who wrote and have memories of those who stepped up on my doorstep just to say "hello" and offer encouraging support at that time. It is more than a gift; it is a treasure.

I discovered a depth of love and forgiveness from my wife and daughters that was truly a picture of how God operates. Family is family, but when tested like they were and to have them come through a self-induced impact like that was a gift that I treasure each and every day.

I received a new appreciation for how God looks at people who need grace and mercy. Offering second chances is His way of operating. To discover and experience grace firsthand, instead of simply teaching it as a theory, was as refreshing as a cool mist from a waterfall on a hot summer day.

It was a gift to discover my own commitment to not let my life be defined by my past. I found it exciting to explore and think about new opportunities ahead of me. To stay stuck in the mindset that said, "But I was called to be a pastor, nothing else will do," would have been stifling. To step out of that box, look around and say, "Okay, what else is possible?" is a template for how I want to work through any interruption that I may yet encounter in the future.

I could go on and list others, but I think you get the picture. If how we do anything is likely a window into how we do everything, I want to be one that looks for the gifts in any situation as tough as the interruption might be. I want to encourage you to look at life that way as well.

LESSONS LEARNED

1. I have a choice as to how I respond to any interruption that comes in life.

2. While some interruptions have more impact on life than others, it can be refreshing to look for the gifts in any situation, regardless of how devastating the moment may be.

3. To look for gifts from any life-changing interruption can be one way to keep our hearts from freezing up and staying stuck in fear or devastation.

COMPASS POINTS

1. What is one of the most impacting interruptions you have experienced in life?

2. If you intentionally searched for gifts from your interruption, what comes to mind as a result?

3. When you turn from focusing on the loss from the interruption to the gifts received from the interruption, what shifts or changes for you?

Let anyone who thinks he stands take heed lest he fall.

1 Corinthians 10:12

Pain is a built-in reminder that things need attention. Change is necessary. Adjustments are required for healing to take place.

From the Wilderness

There are two kinds of guilt:
the kind that drowns you until you're useless,
and the kind that fires your soul to purpose.

Sabaa Tahir

2

GUILT

One time, as a small boy in grade one, I got caught up in a prank that the bigger boys were plotting. They wanted to fill someone's rubber boot with muddy water from a big mud puddle in the front yard of our school. They were hesitant, and since none of them wanted to do it, I offered to put the boot in and scoop up the water. Without much thought, I did the deed and handed the boot back. I guess I wanted to be a hero in the eyes of the big boys. Just as I did, the owner of the boot came through the door looking for his other boot and immediately sized-up the situation. He turned back inside and called for the teacher.

She came out of the school, stood on the top of the steps with her hands on her hips and demanded, "Who did this?" I stepped behind one of the bigger boys and stood still. He didn't move and no one spoke. She asked again, "Who did this?" I was guilty and I knew it. I stepped out from behind my bodyguard and admitted, "I did!" I was terrified! My ride home pulled up right then and the teacher realized I had to leave so she said she would deal with this the next day.

I had a very restless night, knowing that I could not deny or hide what I had done. I was guilty. I absolutely dreaded going to school the next morning. She said she would talk to me at noon, so in fear and confusion, I had to wait even longer. I sat in silence at my desk and waited all through the noon hour for her to talk to me so that I could take my punishment and go enjoy the sunshine. Five minutes before the noon recess ended she said I could go. The punishment had been that I had to stay inside while my friends played outside on a sunny day. I had nothing to argue or defend. I had acted in a way that could not be denied, and there were consequences.

But that is just a miniscule example in comparison to the turmoil I was in as I began this wilderness journey. I was searching to find my way back to the person I had once been, and I had much to process.

Have you ever done something that makes it really tough to be able to look directly at yourself in the mirror? We are human and we are broken because of the human condition we all possess from birth.

Knowing the choices I had made, I was fully aware of the dark, double life I had been living. I knew that on the inside I was not the person I presented on the outside. I had long since accepted the reality of those destructive choices and that I could never go back and remake them differently. My personal integrity was in tatters, but I was determined that I would live out my days dealing with it all internally. Like a never-ending drumbeat my thoughts pounded: "Where was your head?" "What were you thinking?" "Why did you ignore your soul and conscience?"

My mind would swirl, and my guilt was real. I could not deny its presence. I found that I could look in the mirror, but I couldn't look myself in the eye! I knew too much about myself, and what I knew was incredibly embarrassing and disappointing.

The good thing was that only the one looking in the mirror knew the reality! My family, friends and colleagues did not know, and I was determined they would never find out.

But the fact that I was the only one who knew the truth didn't change the depth of disappointment in myself at what I knew. I believed that if anyone else ever discovered the truth about what I knew about myself, my family would forsake me and probably everyone else would wipe me off their friend list forever and move on to associate with more honorable people. The constant, negative stories I told myself built a wave of fear that was paralyzing.

As I understand the universality of the human condition, I'm sure someone reading these words has been in a place of fear in the past because of something they are fully aware they are guilty of doing. Maybe someone can totally relate to what I am saying and is in a similar place, in some form or fashion, at this very moment. It may not be a similar story to mine that haunts you, but possibly there is some dark secret that may be eating you up from the inside out this very day.

GUILT

I remember a day in high school when the teacher asked us all about our homework and one of my classmates simply said, "I didn't do it." She had no response. His admission was simple and truthful, but there was no emotion around it. He was guilty and he knew it. I can still hear his voice and I remember thinking and realizing that a straight up admission of guilt is much better than trying to make excuses!

The dictionary definition of guilt is "the fact or state of having committed an offense, crime, violation, or wrong, especially against moral or penal law. A feeling of responsibility or remorse for some offense, crime or wrong."

The lesson I learned about guilt in my wilderness was that God uses guilt to reach out to our conscience. He doesn't use it in the attempt to make us more miserable. We are already miserable, and He is fully aware of that. He uses guilt to move us to act in a way that would shift us out of our misery. I was not able to avoid the truth about myself. I could pretend, I could attempt to ignore it, but in the dark of the night when I would lie awake, my soul knew, and I knew that God knew. I was guilty. God was gentle, but He was also unchanging. Thankfully, He doesn't make exceptions when we have compromised our souls, and He didn't for me. Like gravity, consequences are a law unto themselves.

In the Bible, there is a story about some people who brought a woman to Jesus whom they accused of being caught in an adulterous act. They had laws stating that people such as her should be stoned to death. They wanted to see if He agreed and would follow their laws. They knew He was prone to mercy and love and so they wanted to force His hand.

He bent down and wrote some of their sins in the sand. By doing so, He made it known that He was fully aware that all were guilty, and He was letting them know that He knew what they were specifically guilty of doing. Then He simply said to them, "Let him who is without sin among you be the first to throw a stone at her." They dropped their stones and suddenly remembered other pressing matters they needed to attend to. Finally, she was alone with Jesus waiting for the punishment to begin.

He asked where her accusers were, saying, "Has no one condemned you?" She looked around and saw that her accusers had all left. "No one, Lord," she said.

Jesus said, "Neither do I condemn you; Go, and from now on sin no more." (John 8:1-11)

He knew she was guilty. "Go and sin no more" was His way of saying "I know the truth about you." He does not want us to live in a place of guilt. He has a much happier and more fulfilling way for us to live. But "Neither do I condemn you" was His way of saying your guilt is real, but it's what you do with your guilt that matters to me.

The discomfort of guilt is God's way of getting our attention and calling to us to come to Him for freedom and release. It's like the disturbing pebble in our shoe that continually reminds us that something is not right and needs to be dealt with. It stays and festers exactly as long as we continue to ignore it, but it is relentless. As it should be!

Many years ago I read a book by Paul Brand and Philip Yancey called *Pain, The Gift That Nobody Wants.* I was fascinated by that book and learned that while we wince whenever we encounter pain, and therefore avoid it at all cost, we really would do well to look at pain differently. They pointed out that if we had no pain when our feet blistered, we would continue to walk on sores and only make them worse. We would damage tissue and bone should we continue to put pressure on places that are injured and broken.

Pain is a built-in reminder that things need attention. Change is necessary. Adjustments are required for healing to take place. Our nervous system is the pain monitor for our bodies.

Guilt is the pain monitor for the heart and spirit. When guilt works the soul, to ignore it only makes the wound deeper and it will require more attention for healing to do its transforming work.

Just as pain is not pleasant but necessary for the body, guilt is not pleasant but necessary for the soul. It's the Holy Spirit doing His work. Jesus said, "When he [the Holy Spirit] comes, he will convict the world concerning sin and righteousness." John 14:8 That conviction is hard when the human heart wants to go its own way and satisfy its own desires. It's simply God's way of reminding us that if we don't pay attention, we will just do more and more damage.

Instead of seeing guilt as something we should avoid, what if we took a different perspective and realized that it's actually a gift to us? We love gifts. We welcome them. What if we welcomed guilt, and as soon as we noticed it lurking, we took it as a nudge to make the necessary adjustments to relieve the heart discomfort?

His Spirit calls to our spirit to remind us that living a life of integrity with Him is much, much wiser. He reminds us of the beauty and simple joy of living a life with Him, as opposed to the futility of spinning our wheels in a place of regret but doing nothing about it.

This time in the wilderness taught me many lessons. As I processed the truth about guilt, I came to accept with awe and gratitude that my failure was known to God before I even took that turn in the path, and that He loved me as much in the middle of my guilt as He did before anything went wrong. It was an amazing day when I realized that even though He knew the future road ahead of me, He had still called me into pastoral ministry in a very distinct and definite way.

As I remembered and re-read stories of how God dealt with sinners just like me, I was reminded that He was always good to them, and He was always loving. He never turned anyone away who wanted freedom from guilt. Those stories gave me courage. I began to believe that if God could love them, maybe He could also love and forgive me. But that is another lesson and another chapter.

LESSONS LEARNED

1. Just as sand in our shoe creates an irritation to our foot, guilt creates an irritation to our heart and sends the signal that transforming change is necessary in order to find peace and happiness.

2. Guilt is actually a gift that we should welcome, agitating our soul for only one noble reason. To ignore this is to continually deal with the discomfort and agitation until we have had enough and make the changes that need to be made.

COMPASS POINTS

1. Think of areas in your life or decisions you have made in the past that have made you feel guilty. What feelings come up within you when you bring them to mind?

2. Knowing that you can never totally escape these feelings of guilt until you address them head on, what will you do differently?

3. What does it cost you to let guilt remain unaddressed?

NOTES FOR MY BACKPACK

Guilt says, "I've done something bad."
Shame says, "I'm a bad person."
Guilt says, "I told a lie." Shame says, "I'm a liar."

From the Wilderness

Memories from different experiences in life morph into belief systems that can bury us unless we take charge and process them in healing ways.

From the Wilderness

3

SHAME

I have shared how I learned that guilt is a gift from God, calling me to come to Him and realign my values and life with His plan for me. Only then would I know peace and passion for life once again. However, I also learned that shame is a whole different deal. There is a considerable difference between guilt and shame.

The dictionary definition of shame is "the painful feeling arising from the consciousness of something dishonorable, improper, ridiculous, done by oneself or another."

While guilt is more a matter of fact and pushes us toward taking accountability for actions done, shame is centered in emotion and feelings caused by those actions. Guilt is admission and acknowledgement and may or may not carry much emotion. Shame is an emotion magnet and sadly, it attracts only negative emotions.

Guilt says, "I have done something bad." Shame says, "I am a bad person." Guilt says, "I told a lie." Shame says, "I am a liar." Shame attempts to bind us to our past so that we are not free to discover who we really are. Some settle for less than they could be today, but what is even worse is to let shame hold us back from ever moving forward.

To take it even deeper, I came to understand that there is healthy shame and unhealthy shame. Healthy shame is experienced in the presence of loving people who do not minimize the reality and the shamefulness of the situation or actions taken, but in love, choose to walk beside the guilty one and create a safe place for the work to be done to restore the dignity of the person or persons involved. They allow the person to fully express and verbalize their emotions about their guilt and still accept them with dignity and friendship.

Unhealthy shame is the work of an enemy who wants to crush the soul of the guilty one and remove all hope of experiencing any amount of dignity in the future. The heart full of unhealthy shame is the enemy's target in the hope to crush it completely. I experienced both healthy and unhealthy shame.

At the time my secret story came to light, I was a member of a church congregation that became a close circle around me and my family in a whole new way as we journeyed through this experience together. The pastor of the church invited me to a board meeting where I openly acknowledged and apologized for the hurt that I had caused the church. I wrote a letter to the board, offering the removal of my name from church membership.

At the following worship service, I was given an opportunity to speak publicly to the whole congregation. I took the opportunity and acknowledged my inappropriate and sinful behavior and I apologized to everyone present.

Later that evening, the church met together and discussed an appropriate response to my unfolding story. The process that came out of that meeting is what I would call healthy shame. I will explain.

My pastor came to visit after the meeting. I was told that my membership would not be removed but that I was to enter a period of what they called "Intensive Care," a much better description than "Church Discipline," which is what it was. It was firm, but very loving and very gentle.

My membership would be "on hold," in that although I was still a member, I would not be allowed to participate in any form of leadership or up-front presence in the church. I was to be visibly present in church each week unless I was traveling away. This was not meant as punishment, but as a gesture of the congregation to remind us that while we were healing they did not expect anything from me, and the reason for me to be present was to allow them to personally interact with and minister to us as a family.

As a part of the healing process the congregation made a commitment to stay very close to us. The church had created a list of volunteers who committed to step up beside each of us, including my wife and two daughters. They were to check in with us on a regular basis, just to let us know that we were not alone and that we were supported. I was also to meet with my pastor on a regular basis, as he would monitor my growth and commitment to healing.

Also, a couple in the church committed to meet with me and Gwen together on a monthly basis. This gave us an opportunity to share how we were managing the emotion and healing that our relationship was going through.

This whole process, as outlined, was to continue for an entire year, at which time the church would come together again to hear from me and from those who had spent time with us. Another vote would then be taken. If successful, I would again be reinstated to full membership in good and regular standing in the church.

The reality is that the decision to follow certain guidelines for a year was in fact a collective reminder that my actions were shameful, but the whole process was to assure me and my family that we were not standing alone in that shame. This is healing shame. This is what God wants for any of us when we fail to demonstrate the integrity that God calls us to.

After one year, the second meeting took place. An affirming and positive vote was taken. With verbal support from friends and prayer together, my membership was restored to good standing. The very next week I was invited to participate in leadership of the worship service. Healthy shame is a blessing in so many ways.

Around the same time that my membership was reinstated, Gwen and I were invited to participate in a process to determine the possibility of ever being involved in pastoral ministry again at some point in the future. To fulfill one of the requirements, for a period of about six months we met regularly with a small committee of three people, each with expertise in a professional line of work. The first meeting was the hardest as they asked me to share my journey with them. I did not hesitate to be open and honest with them, as difficult as that was.

This group of three wept with us, prayed with us, laughed with us, and loved us. We were all very honest about the truth of the condition of the human heart, and with the seriousness of my story. Nothing was excused, yet there was much forgiveness and never once did I feel judged or condemned. It was truly an experience where I was loved despite the reason we were brought together. This is how it should always be as we encounter people who are living with regret.

On the other hand, unhealthy shame pulls us into a very dark, even terrifying place, where we stumble and fumble around looking for the door that will let us out. Many have been so hopeless they have even taken their own lives. I came to realize that unhealthy shame is the action of an enemy of my soul. It is in no way the work of God.

I would personally experience both healthy shame and unhealthy shame in my wilderness journey.

During the time of my secret life, I believed that should the truth be revealed, and I be forced to face reality with others, that pathway out of my situation would no doubt simply pile shame on top of the shame I was already experiencing. I continued to search for a different way out. I wanted freedom without having to face any consequences. Then, it finally became clear that there was only one exit. This was through the door of confession, which led straight into the consequences of my choices and the subsequent wilderness.

Unhealthy shame is the Devil's way of pushing our poor choices in our face and telling us that we are foolish, stupid, evil, unforgivable people, beyond grace and forgiveness, and forever useless to God. The enemy's shame reminds us constantly that we are too compromised, too broken, and too damaged to even hope for any peace in the future. And his work had a drastic effect on me. I spent a lot of time believing it. I wonder if you have too? I carried my regrets on my sleeve. I talked about them to anyone who would listen. I cried. I avoided people, even good friends. I was overwhelmed and completely consumed by unhealthy shame.

One of the valuable things I learned on the journey was that unhealthy shame teaches us to make up stories about ourselves. We make up those harsh stories from events and memories of our past, which are anchored deeply in our souls. And, these stories are not kind, they are not encouraging, and they seek to destroy the picture of how God sees us. But the worst part of all is that we often come to actually believe these stories to be true.

Those stories grow from a variety of experiences in life. It could be from early childhood, or at any stage of life. Things happen, words are said, parents and friends act or say things and we make up stories about those words and events. Memories from different experiences in life morph into belief systems that can bury us unless we take charge and process them in healing ways.

As I thought back over events from my life, I came to realize that for as long as I could remember, I harbored and held on to a dark thought that I had come to believe was true. I don't even know if I had ever spoken those exact words at any point. It was just a belief that took root at some point and was a story in my subconscious mind. Through an exercise I did one time at a retreat I attended, I realized that I had come to believe that I was simply "a disappointment." When I first articulated those words in that context, they resonated deeply. The story I had allowed myself to believe deep inside was that "I am a disappointment."

I could remember things I had done or said, or things I had not accomplished as well or as quickly as I should have, no doubt disappointing people. I was born with a blood clotting condition that put me in the hospital many times as a child. Those events stressed and worried my parents continually. I was not "normal." I realize now that I no doubt sowed the thought seeds to one day believe that I must have been a disappointment. I'm sure my parents didn't see it that way, but those are the things we take on ourselves

I could think of times I could have been a better parent, or a better pastor. I remembered situations in my ministry that I wish I could do over again because I had messed it up the first time.

And now, my crowning act of shame was known to the world. It all came together, and it was undeniable. I had proven beyond question that I was a disappointment.

Healthy shame says, "You DID IN FACT DO THINGS that disappointed others. Let's restore your soul." Unhealthy shame says, "You truly ARE a disappointment. Just admit it." And the enemy was pleased that I was in such a dark place.

I wonder if you carry any of those dark thoughts of shame around with you? They are designed by the enemy to turn us away from God. They call us to give up and to release hope of any meaningful or peaceful future.

These thoughts could be springing up from current events in life, or from shame that comes from events in the far, distant past. They could be things that no one knows, or they could already be known, but you are still convinced that people judge, scorn or look down on you for them.

Remember, it is an enemy who is planting those thoughts within you. I have good news for you in the pages ahead.

When everything changed in my life and the truth of my life became known, all kinds of fearful things went through my mind. My secret was no longer a secret and so it was easy to believe that everyone I knew was now essentially looking into the mirror with me. I was convinced that all of them, even some I didn't recognize, were all looking at me with piercing eyes. Staring, unflinchingly at me. I was nothing but a big disappointment to all of them and I was afraid I would have very few friends, if any, ever again.

In the days and weeks that followed, there were a few changes, and some things shifted. It seemed as though some were looking with harsh and judgmental eyes, and others showed eyes of pain, hurt and confusion, even sadness, but did not really know what to say or do. Thankfully, there were also those who looked at me with eyes of grace and love. These people were even willing to check in and invest some time to journey with me for a bit on various occasions. They asked questions, expressed encouragement, and made sure I knew that I was not alone.

I had many doubts and confused questions. What was I going to do with all the embarrassment and defeat? How was I ever going to be able to pick my head up and go forward? I didn't want to go anywhere and did not want to see anyone. I became a recluse, spending time only at my house or at the golf course, feeling most comfortable when I could walk the course alone, playing by myself. I spent untold hours alone, just thinking, wrestling with my emotions, and most of all, hiding from the world.

The enemy of souls is quick to work against us, especially when we give him reason and leverage to do so. He had many points of reference to push in my face as he reminded me of my secret journey. I could not argue with him, the facts were all true, so the truth of it all just festered in my soul. It was easy to believe that while other sinners could be forgiven, I was beyond that privilege. That is a very dark place. If you have believed that, or believe it right now as you read this, I want to assure you that this is absolutely false. The lessons I learned on my journey gave me a better perspective and the ability to see with clarity the full and rich life that God wants for every person alive on planet Earth.

LESSONS LEARNED

1. Healthy shame, delivered by loving friends, is an intentionally restorative, healing, and loving process. When done well, it is very refreshing to a hurting heart.

2. Unhealthy shame is the work of an enemy desiring to keep us stuck and unable to live in freedom.

3. Shame attempts to define our character in a negative light instead of addressing the actions themselves.

COMPASS POINTS

1. Where have you bought into the enemy's shame and allowed yourself to believe things about yourself and your character that are not true?

2. What would change for you if you could separate actions you are not proud of from the labels that you put on yourself about those actions?

3. What could you do for others that would provide healing space for them as they process their shame?

Forgiveness is to no longer be the judge of another.
You cannot love someone and
judge them at the same time.

Michelle Jeffrey

When I forgive, I am giving myself the gift of freedom and release from the emotions that sabotage my own peace and freedom of spirit.

From the Wilderness

The first to apologize is the bravest.
The first to forgive is the strongest.
The first to forget is usually the happiest.

Project Forgive

4

FORGIVENESS

When my secret life became known, I completely withdrew from the life with which I was familiar. I was alone, withdrawn, and deep in my own thoughts. This is what I refer to as the wilderness. It was a journey through the dark struggles and the stories I was clarifying in my mind. It was a deep, grinding experience of processing and sorting out my values and my anchor points in order to determine what truth there was for me to grasp and learn from. I was alone and it was a dry place. I thought often of Moses and how he spent about forty years in the wilderness, mostly hanging out with sheep. Forty years provides a lot of time to process life. As one who enjoyed friendships and relationships with many people, this was new and unknown territory for me.

The agenda of the things I needed to sort out was full and very significant. The first task was the work of coming to terms with what this failure meant to God and learning about where I stood with Him.

It was also very urgent to take decisive steps to help heal the damage I had caused my wife, my family, and my friends.

Of course, another challenge that haunted me in the hours I would lay awake at night, was figuring out how to live with myself and be able to look at myself in the mirror again. Early in the journey, I decided I had no choice, and I would just have to haul that semi-trailer-load of regrets with me for the rest of my life. I had sold out my soul, and I would have to live with that truth and deal with it, forever.

While I did in fact experience rejection from some people, I also immediately began to hear from many who contacted me for the sole purpose to simply stand beside me and let me know I was not alone. Word got back to me about some of the hard things a few people were saying about me, but I was grateful and encouraged by those who were quick to offer grace and gentleness for what I was experiencing.

There were many phone calls. Emails came in abundance. Others stopped by. No one excused me, but they made it clear I was still loved and cared about despite it all. I was a bit overwhelmed by that. I didn't expect to be excused, but it was great that these people took time to express love and concern for me. The enemy's shame was strong, and inside I wondered, "How can you love me now when I am so unlovable?"

I accepted, as truth, the assumption that I did not deserve to be excused. The enemy of souls wanted me to be weighted down with the thought that there were consequences to my decisions and actions. I would have to reap what I had sown for the rest of my life. I was prepared to pay that price, and realized that I had no choice but to do so. I just was not sure exactly what that price fully looked like yet. I did not know how much it would cost or how long it would take.

In the process of time, I came to realize what I really wanted in the end. I wanted to be forgiven and I wanted to be assured of that forgiveness. I wanted to know how to forgive myself. Was that possible? Was it even a reasonable hope? Should I dare hope that I could forgive myself, or should I just accept that I must carry these regrets until I die?

My greatest concern was wondering if I would miss Heaven and eternal life because of my decisions and actions. Was it really true that God was a forgiving God? I had preached it many times and counseled others to accept His forgiveness. My unhealthy shame made me wonder if His grace was sufficient for one who had crashed as far and as deeply as I had. I pondered those thoughts and questions as I stumbled along in my wilderness.

What is forgiveness really? What was this forgiveness I was really searching for so intently? What was it about forgiveness that I craved?

I am shocked at some of the stories I have heard in my lifetime that unveil what people have had to experience. Sometimes I am speechless. Human cruelty to other people can be almost unbelievable, and even more shocking when it happens in families. Wounds are left and even though they heal over time, the scar that remains reminds us of the pain that was once inflicted.

Through those stories, I have learned some great lessons about forgiveness. I believe that healing and forgiveness must intersect at some point. Healing cannot happen until forgiveness is experienced. But what does forgiveness look like?

It is crucial to realize that unforgiveness is a very hard pill to swallow. Its bitterness affects everything we say or do. The acid of unforgiveness erodes our hearts and minds as long as we are willing to let it. Unforgiveness never hurts the person we are bitter towards as much as it hurts us. I have watched people live a very hard life only because they are unwilling to forgive a person for some action in their past experience.

I think of a lady who was very hurt by a divorce she experienced. I knew of her and met her once when I was a child. She lived the rest of her life in the cold darkness of bitterness. Her granddaughter told me that her grandmother, on her deathbed, admitted that she had wasted her life in that bitterness. How very sad.

But what does it mean to forgive?

Let me start the answer to that question by talking about what forgiveness is not. Forgiveness will never require one to say, "I know I need to forgive you, so I want you to know that I have finally been able to come to terms with it. I will accept the fact that what you did to me is OK!" It is not necessary, in fact it is even unhealthy, to believe that one must accept and state that it is "ok that you did that to me" in order to be able to forgive! Hurtful and damaging behavior is never acceptable, and it never will be.

It is crazy-making to even think that is what would be required. I could never expect God or my wife or my family or my friends to say, "I've finally come to terms with this and it's OK what you did. I need to forgive you and move on."

Forgiveness is never based on the need to make the hurtful actions or words of another person acceptable. Forgiveness is in fact much more significant than that!

In my wilderness journey, I came to realize that when people were kind to me and stood by me despite knowing the truth about me, they were never saying, "I'm fine with what you did even though you hurt me and a whole lot of people." They were saying, "*In spite of what you did*, and the hurt that your actions have caused me and others, I am not going to remind you of it or seek revenge. I choose to move forward with you even while knowing everything that I now know." That is forgiveness. That is grace.

Forgiveness is not an emotional feeling that one must achieve. It is a choice one makes to let go of bitterness, anger and the need for revenge or payback. It is ludicrous to think that a child would ever have to say to the parent that abused him/her, "I forgive you, it's OK what you did." Abuse, damaging words, stealing, lying, adultery or bad behavior of any kind is never, ever acceptable. However, there is much peace in saying, "I have chosen to forgive you so I will not make this a battlefront between us anymore. We may talk about this again, but I choose not to remind you of it in a hurtful way. I forgive you."

Someone once said, "Bitterness is like swallowing poison hoping the other person gets sick." The poison builds up into anger and festering bitterness that only consumes the one who is unwilling to forgive. The person I am bitter against may even be totally oblivious to what is going on with me. The reality is that when I forgive, I am giving myself the gift of freedom and release from the emotions that sabotage my own peace and freedom of spirit. Forgiveness is the act of poking a hole in that toxic bucket and letting all the poison drain out.

Ironically, the truth is that forgiveness is a gift we give ourselves. It changes nothing about the other person, but it changes everything about the way we feel and the stress we carry in our own souls.

As I broadened my understanding, I processed forgiveness at these four points of need: forgiveness from God, forgiveness from my wife and family, forgiveness from friends, and lastly forgiveness for myself.

I read in the Scripture about God's work of forgiveness as expressed through Jesus Christ.

The Bible story tells us that we were created from a perfect God with a perfect plan. Adam and Eve changed all that when they decided to listen to the enemy who tempted them to doubt God and His plain word of caution. Their children, and all generations since then, including ours, have been affected by their actions. We too have been born with a seed of doubt about God implanted in us. That seed grows to fruition, and we experience it in many ways. It expresses itself continually. We are all in need of forgiveness for this condition of sin that we are born into.

It's just like being born with a terminal illness that our parents cannot heal. Doctors study it, scratch their heads, read the literature and consult with experts, then finally say, "We are at a loss. There is nothing more we can do."

Some are born with a rare disease that doctors cannot heal. However, we are all born with a spiritual disease called sin that will paralyze our souls and destroy God's plan for us. No parent or human can turn that around. But God, in His mercy, wanted to change the finality of that for anyone who desired the remedy for sin. He sent His Son to change all that. We needed a Savior outside of ourselves, and He provided one for us that could meet that very specific need. His provision is for anyone who accepts it, but it takes a decisive choice. He doesn't force Himself or His forgiveness on anyone.

Jesus said it succinctly when He was on earth. "For God so loved the world that he gave his only Son, so that everyone who believes in him will not perish but have eternal life." John 3:16 (NLT)

I have known that text since I was a child. It may have been the first one I memorized. I knew the words, but I was so broken I wasn't sure that it could apply to me after what I had done. I kept reading.

I read about some men who brought their friend to Jesus. This man was paralyzed from the diseases that some suggest were brought on as a result of his lifestyle. Jesus looked at him and said, "My son, your sins are forgiven." Mark 2:5. They brought him to be healed of his physical problem, but Jesus started with his heart problem. Then He healed his legs as well.

Jesus said to the woman caught in the act of adultery, "Neither do I condemn you; go and sin no more." John 8:11 (NKJV)

I read about a woman who washed His feet with her tears and expensive oil, and He said to those nearby, "I tell you her sins—and they are many—have been forgiven, so she has shown me much love." Luke 8:47 (NLT)

I read story after story, and I began to let the stories become my stories. I began to believe that maybe He would say those things to me, too. I longed to hear Him say to me personally, "Bill, I don't condemn you either. Your sins, which are many, are forgiven.

Whosoever believes in me will not perish." And I began to believe that it could apply to me, too. Really believe it, from my heart.

His forgiveness was not, "It's OK what you did, I forgive you." It was more like, "It's not OK what you did, but that is why my Son went to earth. His mission was to live the life you were not able to live, teach the truth about life, love, and forgiveness, and die the death you were destined to die. If you believe in Him and that He truly was the Son of God who did all this, you will have eternal life." In other words, "In spite of what you have done, I forgive you."

Along with those stories, I became more aware of the fact that the stories of the Bible involved people who messed up their lives and yet were written for us as examples. While Joseph and Daniel are the only two Bible characters whose stories don't include a dark chapter of failure, we can be sure that they were not perfect people either.

Many other stories speak about failure, sometimes at horrific expense. David committed adultery and then had the woman's husband murdered to try to hide his actions, yet he is the most revered king in all ancient Israel. Saul hunted Christians before he was converted and wrote half of the New Testament. Jacob had two wives and two servants who birthed children for him creating a lot of family drama and pain. He was the grandson of Abraham and was the father of the twelve tribes of the Jewish nation which gave birth to Jesus Himself. These and several more examples told me that God offers second chances and uses broken people for good in His kingdom.

I read in Romans 8:39 that, "For I am sure that neither death nor life, nor angels nor rulers, nor things present nor things to come, nor powers, nor height nor depth, nor anything else in all creation will be able to separate us from the love of God in Christ Jesus our Lord."

As I thought about that text, I realized that my sin and actions were not beyond the scope of God's love. If those things could not separate me from God, then my sin did not either. That was a very reassuring thought.

Early in my wilderness journey I read a book called *Rebuilding Your Broken World,* by Gordon MacDonald. It's his story, a pastor, on a journey very similar to mine. In the book he expressed the thought that our sins are not a surprise to God, who knows everything about our past, present and future. He knows the seed of sin that we are born with, and He understands how it works. Our mistakes do not catch Him off guard. That thought resonated deeply within me.

I believe that my call to ministry was personal, specific, and very real. When I read MacDonald's thoughts, I realized that God called me to ministry knowing my future and how my actions would in fact hurt Him, hurt many and damage many people's trust in pastors. I was amazed and very humbled that, despite what He saw coming in the future for me, He had called me anyway.

Somewhere, in all those stories and events I was able to say out loud to Him that I believed Him. I finally and fully accepted that His forgiveness was for me, too. And I accepted that He would not condemn me for my life and actions. The light at the end of the tunnel was getting a little brighter.

My daughters went through their own process of healing. I am not intimately privy to all that they experienced. We have talked together, but I respected their privacy and did not pry beyond what they have been willing to share. I just know, that as a family, we worked to rebuild and to heal. We continued to do things together and became close as we moved through those dark days. I felt their love and forgiveness despite their pain. I am aware that my actions cost them much, but I also have enjoyed their forgiveness, love, and grace toward me.

I experienced forgiving love from Gwen very quickly. She was hurt in ways that I cannot fully know the depth of. Her tears were hot and burning. Her emotions were real, raw, and fair. I could not dodge them, neither did I try. I was fully aware and acknowledged that I was the cause of her pain, and I could not ask her to just "get over it." I knew that her grief needed time and a safe space to process and bring the healing we were both looking for. I answered her questions and I never rushed her or asked her to stop talking about whatever she needed to talk about.

Through time and process, with continued counseling, we experienced healing in our marriage. The pain I caused her was never, ever going to be OK, and I was never going to minimize it to her. I was open with her and would forever be aware of what my actions had done to someone I loved. She had loved and believed in me and did not deserve the consequences she also had to experience. In the beauty and love that forgiveness brings, she has been able to love me despite the pain I caused her. She does not condemn me or hold it over me in harsh or negative ways. She seeks no revenge. Forgiveness does that in spite of everything, and she demonstrates it continually.

And, as those I knew continued to speak kindly to me, I was able to face life, people, and friends again. Each gesture of love was an act of forgiveness and the statement of their willingness to let the story rest. They were in fact offering the very thing I craved, forgiveness, but I was not yet able to fully accept it or take it in. It was one slow step after another toward the light at the end of a long, dark tunnel.

I remember an event that took place within the very first week after my secret became known. Everything was very fresh, and I lived in a constant state of embarrassment. A friend called to invite me for a game of golf and when I met him there, before we began to play he asked, "I hear you have had a hard week. What can I do for you?" I was touched and simply said, "Just treat me like you have always treated me." He said, "Okay! Let's play golf!" He never that day, or since, reminded me of my poor choices. He knew that I was already paying the consequences and he let it go. He had already forgiven me.

I have told you what my pastor and my church did for me to offer healing forgiveness. Expressions of forgiveness came to me from so many. It was a very humbling and emotional time.

But there was still one more giant step I needed to take. It was wonderfully sweet that God, my wife, daughters, family and friends, my pastor and my church could demonstrate and express forgiveness toward me, but I struggled deeply with how to forgive myself. That was a prison of a whole different kind. Those regrets were still front and center in my mind. I was resigning myself to the fact it was something that I would have to live with forever.

I questioned my ability, or even my right, to live without regret. How could I ever look at myself in the mirror again and even accept, let alone love the person I saw? I wondered if it was even possible to forgive myself. However, in a truly life-changing moment, one question was asked of me that was the first step to changing everything.

About seven months after our lives changed so drastically, my wife, Gwen, and I attended a life skills workshop called *Choices*. When our personal marriage story became known to the whole group, the facilitator had a short dialog with me in the presence of the one hundred or so people in the room.

She asked me, "How are you?" I answered, "I pull behind me a semi-trailer-load of regrets."

She responded and simply asked, "Well, why don't you unhook it?"

I was startled, and somewhat speechless. I'm sure I answered her, but I don't remember what I said. In my mind I was thinking, and asking myself, "I can actually do that? I can unhook that trailer and not pull it with me for the rest of my life?" It was a thought that I had not entertained, ever. I was sure that I would spend the rest of my life in shame and regret. I had spent months pondering whether that release was truly possible.

That simple question, "Why don't you unhook it?" was the opening wedge to freedom from all my regrets.

I accepted the definition that forgiveness was letting go of all rights to revenge. I also learned at *Choices* that forgiveness is a gift I give myself. I allowed myself to receive the forgiveness of God, Gwen, and my daughters. I allowed myself to receive the forgiveness of friends. And each time I accepted that forgiveness I moved closer to receiving my own forgiveness.

In due time, in my wilderness of thought, healing and learning, I put the forgiveness pieces together. God can forgive me and not seek revenge or condemn me. My wife can forgive me and not seek revenge or condemn me. My daughters are not expressing their anger and need for revenge to me. Many friends are stepping up and treating me lovingly and kindly. What if I did to myself what everyone else is doing to me and let go of my bitterness toward myself? It was never going to be OK, but what if I let myself off the hook for all the things I had said and done?

I could not think of one thing that anyone in my life could do that I would not readily forgive them for if they asked me to. I am not one for holding grudges. If my closest friend, wife, or parent came to me and said, "I need your forgiveness for….", I know that there would be no need to discuss it further. Sincere apology goes deep with me, and forgiveness would easily be put into place and we could move ahead.

So, if I could do that for anyone else, why could I not offer that to myself? I decided that I actually could. What a day that was!

Freedom came to me. Peace became a reality that I experienced on a regular and steady basis. I was no less guilty of the actions that had caused all the pain, but people were loving me and accepting me anyway. I could never explain away, make excuses, or make my actions right, nor would I try. But I could in fact turn my thoughts forward, live in a place of forgiveness of myself and stop beating on my own heart and soul. I needed to stop taking out revenge on myself and letting my regrets control my thoughts and my days. I finally decided to love and accept myself despite that, too. I was finally experiencing forgiveness in the true sense of the word.

People often say that forgiveness and forgetting go together. "You must forgive and forget!" I believe it's impossible to forget significant negative events and choices that we encounter in life. Those that we make, or those that are made by others that personally impact us. How could I be expected to forget how I had let myself down so far and started this journey?

I heard a story about Clara Barton, the lady who founded the Red Cross. Someone reminded her about a very cruel thing someone had done to her and was amazed that Clara could not remember that. "How could you not remember that, it was in all the newspapers?" Clara responded by saying, "I distinctly remember forgetting that."

I have read many great statements on the internet that caught my attention and got me thinking. This one kind of sums up what I'm saying. From a group called Project Forgive I read, "The first to apologize is the bravest. The first to forgive is the strongest. The first to forget is usually the happiest."

I have learned that forgiveness trumps forgetting. When we remember something that was done to us, it does not cause further grief because forgiveness makes it possible to distinctly remember forgetting it.

Two things helped me to do that. First, was to fully believe and accept the truth that God had forgiven me. Truly forgiven. He forgave me before I made the poor choices. He forgave me while it was still a secret. He forgave me and still forgives me to this day. He holds no revenge or bitterness, only sadness for all involved. While His forgiveness was fully in place and available all that time, I was the one who had to accept it within myself and let it do the work of transforming my entire life. When I truly and fully accepted that, a light as bright as the sunshine flooded my soul.

Secondly, the act of believing and fully accepting the forgiveness of others helped me take one slow step after another toward forgiving myself. As long as I minimized their kind words, I hindered my ability to experience their full forgiveness. I began to really accept that someone could express forgiveness to me, and truly believe they meant it. When forgiveness settles into the soul, it does marvelous healing work. I realized that in that same way, I could forgive and accept myself again, too. I learned to "piggyback" my own forgiveness of myself onto their forgiveness of me. Each time I accepted forgiveness from somewhere else, I would let a piece of my revenge against myself go, too.

Maybe you were one of those who helped me by not letting anger or bitterness get in the way of expressing your forgiveness and acceptance of me. If so, bless you. You helped me more than you can imagine.

I still accept that what I did will never be excusable. Time will never make the pain I inflicted on others acceptable. However, as I choose whether or not to hold myself hostage to my past, each one chooses whether they will hold themselves hostage to their past. We can help each other do that by offering the freedom that comes with true forgiveness. By reaching out in forgiveness we are possibly helping someone find that incredible gift for themselves and step forward into that freedom that God wants us to experience. Why would we not want to do that?

LESSONS LEARNED

1. Forgiveness is not forcing myself to say, "It is OK what you did to me."

2. Forgiveness is letting go of the need for revenge or holding another person hostage because of their actions.

3. Forgiveness of others is a gift we give ourselves because it removes bitterness from our heart.

4. Forgiveness from others, especially from God, gives courage to the broken soul that is plagued with regret and unhealthy shame.

5. Forgiveness from others and from God, gives us permission to forgive ourselves and to let go of any reason to stay stuck there.

6. When we have truly forgiven, we move beyond the need to forget. If we remember a hurtful event from the past, it doesn't matter because forgiveness neutralizes that memory.

COMPASS POINTS

1. Who do you need to forgive so that the bitterness of anger and revenge can drain out of your soul and bring you peace?

2. Who do you need to forgive so they can be released to find joy and freedom?

3. What do you truly need to forgive yourself for?

4. What steps will you take to have all the joy and freedom that is available?

FORGIVENESS

NOTES FOR MY BACKPACK

God is not honored when we are
bound by the memory of the things
He has already forgiven.

From the Wilderness

You can't reach for anything new
if your hands are full of yesterday's junk.

Louise Smith

5

THE HIGH ROAD TO FREEDOM

In October of 2007, I was enrolled in a leadership training course offered by the same company from which I took my Life Coach training. The program consisted of four separate retreats, held at a quiet place located in the Redwoods, just North of San Francisco, California. I attended because I wanted to experience more learning opportunities that would stretch and challenge me.

Part of the course requirement involved participation in high rope exercises. I had signed all the papers that stated I would not hold the organization liable should I fall and hurt or kill myself! We had been told what to bring in preparation for this event, so it was no surprise. I was tentatively excited about the opportunity and learning it would bring.

I had been on a high-rope apparatus once before, so I had a sense of what this challenge was going to look like. I am not one that is comfortable with heights; I get nervous when my socks are a little too thick! When I had signed up for this course, I knew that I would be stretched in new ways. I was confident that I had prepared myself mentally for what I was to experience that first day in the woods. I was sure that I would be fine. I soon realized I had much more to learn.

There were twenty-four of us in the group. The sunshine was warm as we laughed and chattered our way down the hill into the massive Redwood trees. When we arrived at our first stop, I looked around to discover what we would be doing. We were divided into two groups of twelve and the other group went off somewhere, but I paid no attention to where they went as I was fixated on what was in front of me.

Part 1: Falling Free

There was a ladder propped against the trunk of a tree. Above the top of the ladder was a series of well-placed, strong iron staples driven firmly into the tree, big and solid enough to grab onto or step on as we climbed. My eyes traveled up, which seemed like forever, to a place where I saw a rope ladder attached to a platform and stretched out level between two trees. The trees were tall and solid. The ropes on the ladder were strong and well-secured, with another platform to step onto at the other end. The rungs were spaced evenly, but it was anything but stable and sturdy. It didn't take long to figure out that the goal was to climb the tree and walk across that unstable ladder from platform to platform. It was warm, and the sun sprinkled light patches all around us, but I came to the realization that I was shivering and barely breathing. Did I mention that it was at least 30 feet off the ground?

I volunteered to go first. I wanted to get this over with and watch the others with the pressure off me. It had nothing to do with bravery; it had everything to do with, "Let's get this behind me so I can relax!"

I strapped myself into a harness that was also strong and secure. On the front of my harness was a solid ring attached to a rope that looped up through pulleys high above the ladder itself. The clips were sturdy, and the rope was more than capable of catching me should I fall. A team of people held the rope in a system on the ground keeping it tight between myself and them, so that in case I should fall I would be caught very quickly. With my helmet firmly in place and gloves on my hands, I took a deep breath and wondered why I had thought going first was such a good idea.

Amid the enthusiasm of my new friends, I started up the ladder that was leaning against the tree. I reached the top of the ladder, and from there continued to climb the rest of the way up the metal staples that had been driven into the tree.

As I said, heights and I don't get along well, so I kept talking to myself, reminding myself not to look down, and to just take one step at a time. My head told me that if I fell, I would be caught by the rope on my harness and safely lowered to the ground, yet in my heart there was a mixture of excitement and serious apprehension!

I was surprised that the climb seemed almost effortless. In a matter of a minute or two, I was standing on the platform with this unstable ladder laid out in front of me. All I had to do was walk across it. The rungs were spaced about a foot and a half apart, and the ropes on either side would wobble and bounce with each step I took. There was someone standing on the platform on the other side to coach and guide me across.

He encouraged me to take the first step and said, "Your body knows how to find balance. Don't worry about that. Keep your eyes focused on me. Don't look down."

It took about one second to master the "don't look down" part! The rest, I was not so sure of. The rope that secured me was attached to a ring on the front of my harness where I could see it. I took the first faltering step and realized that in order to take the next step, I also had to let go of the tree. I wasn't quite sure how I was ever going to do both of those at the same time. I was still trying to figure out why I had wanted to go first and why I wanted to learn whatever it was I was going to learn up there. Suddenly, it was very clear to me that this was a really dumb idea. Did I mention it was at least 30 feet in the air? And now I was up here on that ladder, not on the ground looking up at it!

I soon realized that if I just looked at the next step, and not all the way to the ground, it really was easy to ignore how high up I was. I also learned that my body really did know how to balance itself, just like the coach had said. Step by step I moved across that ladder until he reached out his hand and helped me up onto the landing on the other side. My friends below were cheering me on. It was exhilarating to realize what I had just accomplished. I was still breathing and doing quite well!

Then the coach said, "You have two options for getting down. You can step off this platform and they will let you down slowly by the rope you are strapped to, or you can attach yourself to this swing and unhook yourself from that rope, and let yourself enjoy the ride. When the swing stops, you will be close enough to the ground to climb down a stepladder!"

I want to tell you that neither of those options sounded particularly appealing! Stepping off a thirty-foot high platform into thin air and trusting the guys at the bottom to hold the rope sounded a bit risky. I loved swinging on the school playground as a kid, but from thirty feet in the air, straight out into nowhere would definitely be a swing unlike anything I had ever experienced before!

I decided on the swing. The coach sat me down on the edge of the platform, and by then, the next person was ready to cross the ladder behind me, so it was time to move on. He hooked the swing rope to my harness, and said, "When you are ready, just hold on to this rope in front of you, lean forward and gravity will take over. You will be fine."

Then he stopped me and said, "Before you go, what would you like to symbolically and emotionally leave here on this platform so that when you swing off into the ride ahead you aren't carrying it with you anymore, and you can be free of it—forever?"

What a fabulous question! I wanted to leave behind all the regrets I carried for my poor choices that still rose up and tormented me from time to time! I wanted to leave behind the fear that I would never be free of them. I wanted to leave behind all the harsh things I had said to myself. How great it would be to leave behind the old story of how I had defined myself as a failure.

I articulated those things to my new friend who just listened without judgment or criticism. Then he said, "So, when you swing, you can leave all that here on the platform and never come back to pick any of it up again. Now, what will you be swinging into?"

I simply said, "A future of freedom from the grinding regrets that keep me stuck!"

"Then, go for it!" he encouraged.

I looked at him and smiled, struck with wonder at the thought of how amazing that would be. I grabbed the rope, closed my eyes and leaned forward. Gravity did indeed do its work! In an instant, I was away and flying free!

I cannot describe the rush that swing brought. For a very brief second, my heart skipped as I shrieked, and then I began laughing in my excitement! It truly was just like being on a swing, just a very big and high one. A swing that I could not fall from. The harness was strong and there was no fear. I didn't want it to end. It was my version of parachuting or flying.

As great as the exhilaration of literally flying and swinging through the air was, I was just as excited at the symbolism created from the discussion that coach and I had just had. I was swinging away from the regret of my past. I could not erase the past or alter it in any way, but neither did I have to live in the dark shadow of it forever. I was swinging into the freedom of the future and the beautiful life that God was creating for me and with me. God is not honored when we are bound by the memory of the things He has already forgiven.

That question on that platform was deeply personal and real to me. So was my answer. When the swing stopped and I was once again standing on the ground, I looked up. I could only see the platform I had just left from the bottom. I knew that I had mentally unloaded a lot of negative stuff that I did not need or want to carry for even one more day. I had left it way up there; in a place I would never visit again. The impact of the choice to fly on the swing was a metaphor for me that truly added up to a new freedom that I only wanted more of.

That day in the woods, after I was safe on the ground, the group leader suggested I go for a short walk in the woods alone to process and journal my thoughts about it all. That day I asked God to let the freedom I was moving into be more than a metaphor. I asked that it be a real, continual, life-long experience! I remembered that Jesus had said in John 8:36, "So if the Son sets you free, you will be free indeed." I had just tasted that freedom in a tangible way and wanted the full freedom that He offered to stay with me as long as I lived.

I'm not the only one who has had to manage regrets. I'm sure that everyone does at some time or another. Even Willie Nelson! I'm guessing he speaks for all of us when he sings his song called *"The Sands of Time."* He asks about what to do with the box full of old regrets that we keep just under our beds.

A lady named Louise Smith is quoted to say, "You can't reach for anything new if your hands are full of yesterday's junk." How true. I was never going to be free from the reality of my past decisions, but I did not need to live the rest of my life in the shadow of the regret of them. To hold on to regret, fear, anger, guilt and shame would only keep me stuck in a very dark place.

Several years later, I was having lunch with a very good friend who had been a fellow pastor and leader. He said, "Sometimes I think about what might have been for you Bill." I quickly responded, "Yes, I do too, but let's not talk about that. It only takes me places that pull me back into my regrets." I wanted those to stay up there on the platform and did not ever want to bring them down to rehearse them even one more time.

Our best moments in life are the experiences we look back on and see where we have overcome our challenges and found freedom. Especially if the struggle has been long and hard. Often, that memory includes people who have seen us at our worst, in our fearful moments, and loved us by offering encouragement and support when we least believed in ourselves. They have not left us when we have been exposed in our most vulnerable ways. When the smoke clears, there they are, where they have been all along.

The power of being the person who breaks free is invigorating. And the gift we are to others by being that support person is equally powerful. The coach who sat with me on that platform impacted my life through the questions he asked. Then, he did not dig or drill, he just sat and listened, and encouraged me to "Go for it!" We can be important to someone most every day of our lives. True friends stand by us until we are able to swing into the freedom that awaits us.

Part 2: Jumping Out of Trees

As incredible as that experience was, I was not prepared whatsoever for what was yet waiting for me that very same day. After everyone had taken a turn on the ladder and swing, we had a lunch break and then moved on to another adventure. Our two groups swapped places and while they went to walk the ladder, our group went to see what they had been up to.

We took a different path that came to another tree. Like the previous one, the ladder only went part way up, and then gave way to the same familiar staples to get us from the top of the ladder and on up to a platform. This platform was, again, about thirty feet in the air. In many ways it was very familiar, and then it was terrifyingly different.

Instead of a rope ladder on the edge of this platform, there was a plank. It was a diving board! It was not attached to another tree; it just jutted out and then simply ended. It didn't take long for me to figure out what was expected here. Climb the tree, get on the platform, walk the plank, and step off into thin air. No pool of water below, just a rope to hold you and let you down. Simple!

My next response, to whomever was standing nearby, was "Not a chance. I may look like a chicken, and I may embarrass myself by refusing to go, but I am not going to do that!"

Immediately, members of the group began to encourage me and challenge me, saying that everyone else would be doing it, and I could, too. I was adamant that I would watch and cheer them on, but I would be staying on the ground.

I watched the first person go. He was a classic example of fear and bravery all rolled into one, but he did it, and survived.

They continued to encourage me, and I began to entertain the thought that maybe I could do this. Finally, one said, "Bill, if I can do it, you can do it, too!" I continued watching, and I continued to consider it. Another four or five people went and all survived quite nicely. I finally concluded that yes, I could do this, too. Taking a deep breath when it was my turn, I strapped that harness on, attached the safety rope, and started up the tree. The difference this time, was that the rope was attached to my harness on the back instead of on the front like the first climb. I could not see it or hold on to it.

I reached the platform quite quickly and crawled on. That was the easy part. I stood up and kissed the tree! It was stable and steady, my last anchor. I slowly turned to face the plank and the never-ending space beyond the end of it.

I have a video of me walking that plank. The picture of the fear on my face could nicely be put in the dictionary next to the word "terror," and it would be the perfect description! I slowly inched my way out onto the plank, trusting that the rope was firmly clipped to my harness and that my harness was firmly strapped and clipped to me. I got to the end of the plank and said to myself, "It's show time!" I stepped off the edge in a motion that was more like an awkward, floating fall outward. There was no water at the bottom if the rope did not hold.

I might have fallen a foot at the most, and it was over. The rope caught me quickly and there I dangled as they lowered me to the ground. Once again, I cannot explain the exhilaration of knowing that I had looked my fear of heights square in the face and won! I was laughing and trembling, and my friends were cheering and clapping as I arrived back on the ground.

Again, I went for a short walk away from everyone else and sat to write in a journal. I have these words to remind me of that moment. "I just leaped off a diving board thirty feet in the air, into thin air---strapped well onto my back where I could not see my security and support. I DID IT! I DID IT! I DID IT!" Then I added, "God, please keep my strength in You keen and alive to face all things!"

The fact that I had adamantly said I would not do it, but then experiencing the exhilaration of actually going ahead and doing it, was a great insight for me. Since that day, when I have faced hard moments in life, facing tasks that I did not want to do, I have remembered that moment. More than once I have said to myself when I have been facing difficult tasks, "If I can jump off a diving board into thin air at thirty feet, I can do this!" And then I move ahead with courage.

Sometimes we face challenges that make us wonder how we will ever be able to move ahead. In the Bible, the Apostle Paul said, "I can do all things through Christ who strengthens me." Philippians 4:13 (NKJV)

That means I can stand for Him. I can follow His plan for me, which prompts me to the healthy service of others. I can do challenging things. I can forgive others. I can forgive myself. I can encourage others when they fail and fall. If I can jump out of a tree, I can do whatever I might need to do for others and for Him.

That day in the woods, climbing, swinging, and jumping out of trees, will forever be a highlight of my life because of the realization I gained from pushing my fear out of the way and doing the task before me. The experience of accomplishment in the face of determined refusal is a memory that will never leave me.

LESSONS LEARNED

1. We can challenge our fears and win if we set our minds to it.

2. We can find balance in very precarious places in life if we will just stop, breathe and focus.

3. We do not have to carry our regrets with us even one more day and let them steal our joy and freedom.

4. The fear of falling is a state of mind. The harness, clips and ropes made it impossible to fall. Most fears are the result of ignoring the evidence around us.

5. Fears must be faced head on. Even after deciding to face my fears, I still had to strap on the harness, climb the ladder and step off the board.

6. Facing our fears helps us realize we can do things we might have previously concluded were impossible.

COMPASS POINTS

1. What fears do you carry that keep you paralyzed?

2. What do you need to do right now in the middle of whatever you might be facing to take even one faltering step forward?

3. What regrets and pain from your past do you really need to put down and leave behind?

4. Imagine your own "platform" where you can leave your regrets once and for all. When will you go to that place and find the freedom it will bring?

5. What picture of freedom comes to you as you leave those regrets behind you.

We would do well to be gracious with people, especially if we don't know anything about their story.

From the Wilderness

The voyage of discovery is not in seeking new landscapes but in having new eyes.

Marcel Proust

6

SEEING WITH NEW EYES

I was on a golf course, playing with two friends along with a gentleman that none of us had ever met before. It was just a few weeks after I had resigned from my pastoral work and entered my wilderness. Things were still very raw for me. I had no idea what the next days, months, or years would look like. I had been searching for employment opportunities that would pay my bills, and yet, would also be fulfilling. I had found nothing. I was disoriented, unsettled, and shaken.

I can still remember where we stood, waiting on the golf course, when the man I had not met before casually asked me, "So, Bill, what do you do?" I responded and said, "Well, I used to be a pastor, but I am not working right now. I am in transition at the moment and I'm not sure what I will be doing."

I don't remember his response, but it was short. Finally we walked on, and a few minutes later he walked up beside me again and said, "I have been thinking about the comment that you are in transition. Have you ever thought of working in the area of mediation?"

"What's mediation?" I asked. I had no idea.

He responded by saying, "I'm a Family Law lawyer. Yesterday I sat with a client of mine and his brother who tried mediation instead of going to court. I didn't think a resolution was even remotely possible, but at the end of the meeting they shook hands and had a very satisfactory agreement in place. I was amazed. I think your pastoral background might set you up wonderfully for that."

It resonated immediately in my mind. Was this something I could pursue? I was excited, and when I finished my golf game, I called Gwen from the club house. I couldn't even wait to get home to tell her what had happened. I exclaimed excitedly, "I believe God showed up on the golf course today. I think I have an idea about what I could do for a new career!" I went straight home to my computer to start finding out more about what it would take. Within a couple of days I was enrolled, and two months later I was sitting in my first class to study conflict resolution and mediation.

As I walked the halls of Grant MacEwan College where I took my classes, everything was new and unfamiliar. I was rubbing shoulders with students the age of my own daughters. I was eating meals in a cafeteria where I didn't know a soul. I was taking classes with people who had a variety of backgrounds and purposes for studying mediation. None of it was familiar. Like Moses, I was in a completely new world, and I kept asking myself, "How did I end up here?"

However, while I was in those conflict resolution classes, I learned new and valuable tools and skills for serving people. Part of the curriculum included mediation role plays with each other. With practice, it became easier to look behind the items that people often argued about and discover the unspoken needs that were driving those conflicts. Rather than just address the surface points of discussion, they taught us to go deeper and discover what the foundational issues were.

For example, two people may argue about a discrepancy in how much money someone owes another person. They can get into quite a heated debate. However, when we ask more questions, it becomes evident that it is not about the money at all. It may be about a fear that they will not be able to financially meet their needs, and this money would help them feel more secure. It could be about respect, believing that "if you respect me, you will give me the amount you owe me without argument."

Or it could be about control, and one might proclaim, "They always think they can run my life and I'm not going to be a doormat anymore. I've given in and done it their way long enough." So, it's not really about the dollar value; that just has become the topic for the next battle. If one focuses only on the money that is being argued over, they might miss the deeper issue completely. Once we uncover that, we can then address the issues of respect and conflict.

When people feel respected and that they have a voice that is being listened to, suddenly the amount of money owed is not nearly as important as it once was. We call it a paradigm shift. Seeing the situation from a new vantage point.

Stephen Covey told a story in his book, *The 7 Habits of Highly Effective People,* about a man and his children who came onto the transit system in a large city. The father slumped down in his chair and was oblivious to the noise and disruption his children were causing to the other passengers around him. Finally, one of the passengers spoke to the father about it and asked him if he realized the trouble his children were causing. The man roused himself and revealed that they were coming from the hospital where his wife, the children's mother, had just died, and he didn't know what he was going to do. He guessed the kids were going through a lot right now as well. The passenger suddenly had a whole new way of looking at that situation and engaged in an empathetic conversation with him. It was a major paradigm shift, seeing the situation from a completely different perspective.

I began to realize, as I was taking those classes, that many things in life, when viewed from one perspective, looked very different when viewed from an alternative one. As I reflected on my life, I had to admit that I had spent a lot of my life judging some people's behaviors and actions instead of attempting to understand things at a deeper level, or from their perspective.

For example, I realized that I had choices. I could look with condescension or judgment on someone, or I could look with curiosity on that very same person. I could move from, "How could you be so irresponsible?" to "Can you tell me about the reasons and thoughts which brought you to that decision?" It's a very different approach and much more constructive. People interact with others much better when they feel respected and engaged, rather than judged or criticized.

Besides judging, I had to admit I was also very good at making assumptions that I really didn't have the right to make. We humans are often assumption-making machines, thinking that we know things about people and why they do certain things, when in reality we are assuming much of what we think is true. The truth is, we don't know as much as we think we do about other people, and we cannot get into their minds to know what they are thinking or determine what motivates them to do the things they do. We would do well to be gracious with people, especially if we don't know anything about their story.

It was great to learn that I could choose empathy for people, rather than blame people or draw unfair conclusions about them. I could work to help them create a better future and plan the next steps with them, as opposed to searching to find who was to blame for the current situation.

It is much more rewarding to observe the impact when people work to solve the issues that divide them, rather than choose to remain adversaries and be stuck in the continual attempt to prove who is right or wrong.

And the best part of it all was how to apply all this learning personally. I realized that I could choose the way I wanted to view people. Putting labels on them didn't define who they really were. I could choose a whole different way of viewing life circumstances, and the people in my life, if I wanted to.

Many ideas began to open up in my mind. What might change for me, and all of us, if we would step back and see the bigger picture about our personal lives, rather than just the current circumstances we find ourselves in? What might change if we would step back and see the bigger picture in the lives of others rather than the circumstances they find themselves in?

One time, I was talking with a gentleman who was telling me about challenges in his marriage. His wife was leaving him because she felt he was too controlling and that she did not have a voice in the marriage.

As I listened to him, I asked him about his father and how his father treated his mother. He spoke about how she had to beg for every dollar he gave her to simply buy food and necessities. He did not like the way his father controlled her. I then asked, "Did you know your dad's father, your grandfather?" He thought for a very brief moment and then his eyes lit up and he quickly blurted out, "Oh yes, he was even worse. My grandmother had no voice at all!"

It was easy to point out that these were the role models of marriage that he had witnessed and learned as a teenager and young adult. He was following in the footsteps of what he had observed as the only way to be in a marriage. I suggested that he could be the one to change the pattern. Just because he was simply living out what he had been taught, didn't mean he had to continue to do it, especially when it was not creating a healthy relationship with his wife. He realized the truth of what I was saying, and we began to discuss ways he could go home and do things differently.

We could have spent much time just focusing on his behavior, but seeing the bigger picture added a dimension to his understanding of why he was living out a marriage that was crumbling around him. Seeing different perspectives can change many things.

So, with those insights coming into my mind, instead of walking the unfamiliar halls of a college I had never been in, and berating myself for being there, I could say, "What are the gifts that I can identify as a result of this sudden change in my life? What is the benefit I can take away from being here?" It didn't take long to really get excited about the opportunity that was actually a blessing for me during this wilderness journey. I remember thinking, "This is so good. Every pastor should have to take these classes to be better able to understand personality, conflict and perspective."

We would do well to search and find more than one way to look at life and the experiences we face. I'm well aware that wilderness settings and dry times can be heavy and dreary. They can also be full of curiosity, wonderment and learning. It's how we choose to experience them. My journey was helping me learn that lesson from many different angles.

In mediation training, when we would search for deeper learning; we called it moving from positions to interests. People come into conflict knowing exactly what they want or what they believe and declare, "This is my bottom line, and I'm not changing it." That's their position. But what drives that position? What is the "interest" behind this position that we are discussing or arguing over? The answer to that is always related to our value systems, and which basic needs, hopes, concerns, and fears are being threatened.

Everyone has a value system they are trying to protect. Conflict is simply the clash of value systems. When we can learn to clearly express our values and also carefully listen as others express theirs, peace and harmony can be restored much more easily. If every one of us would seek to assure that others get to honor their personal values, conflict among us would be virtually wiped out completely.

A personal encounter gave me a perfect word picture to explain this. In talking to a counselor one time, it was pointed out that life is often like looking through a variety of windows. We look at one event through our window, which is a metaphor for our values and our experiences. It may include our judgments and our worldview. Others look at the exact same event from their window, which of course is through their values, experiences, judgments and worldview.

Thinking others are wrong just because they don't see what I see from my window may simply be because I don't stand with them at their window to see exactly what they are seeing. Even a slight shift in angle can change everything. The view from our window only allows us to partially see what another is looking at, and if we saw the totality of what they were viewing from where they stood, it could shift things dramatically. It's so important to take time to look through each other's windows as much as we are able to.

There was lots of time to process the things I was learning. As much as I was enjoying pursuing a new career, I also realized there were important personal lessons here as well. It wasn't just looking out from other windows to help in relationship matters with others, it became obvious that I could look at my own personal life from different windows, too.

I could choose to see my life as a whole and see the big, full picture of the way God had led, and been present with me, even through dark times. I could also choose to move to the next window and to focus just on the hard times of my life. That could be pretty depressing, and could quickly move me to a place of anger at myself. And if I stayed staring out of that window it could easily move me to a place where I would seek out and choose to blame circumstances, or others, for why things were the way they were in my life. I could be angry that I was in the wilderness at all. All because of the window I chose to view my life through.

On the other hand, I had the option of looking through a window of curiosity, reflection and accountability about my personal decisions and choices that had caused me to end up in these circumstances. I could take the position of a learner, seeking to understand the steps that brought me to the wilderness, and what I needed to address there.

We can be hard on ourselves if we only have one point of view. We can be hard on others if we only have one point of view. It's by taking time to see what they see that can change things dramatically.

The Bible says that "All have sinned and come short of God's glory." Romans 3:23 When we encounter differences, it would be helpful to step back and look at ourselves, everyone, and everything else from other angles and with new understanding. It takes time, and it means we may have to back away from our need to be right. But it is much more rewarding. It is always wiser to find out what else is involved before coming to conclusions prematurely. Being willing to be open to other perspectives and possibilities can often bring more peace and calm to many situations. We are all right, but only partially. We seldom or even never have the other's full picture. Being gracious to others is a gift that can really calm the waters.

LESSONS LEARNED

1. Be willing to be open to new opportunities and experiences. There is hidden value in every situation.

2. Look for the truth behind words spoken or actions taken. There are always reasons people do or say things.

3. Learn to look at life from the windows of others before making assumptions or judgments about them.

COMPASS POINTS

1. Who in your life do you find it hard to spend time with? What might shift if you could see life from their perspective?

2. How could embracing new perspectives change life for you overall?

3. What are you facing right now that could change dramatically if viewed as an opportunity?

There is an incredible opportunity
awaiting us if we don't ever stop
being curious about "what else" is possible.

From the Wilderness

Pretending everything is okay is never solid ground
on which to base any foundation.

From the Wilderness

7

WE DON'T KNOW WHAT WE DON'T KNOW

Shortly after making the decision to pursue mediation training, I found myself walking the halls of Grant MacEwan College in Edmonton on a fairly regular basis. I made a few friends of the instructors and the other students in the courses I was taking, but most of the people were strangers to me. The people I passed in the hallways and cafeteria were the age of my daughters. I felt out of place and a bit lost many times.

I have always been someone who finds it easy to see the bright side of things. I found that even though I was out of my environment, I really was enjoying the material and skills I was learning. Never in my high school, college or seminary training had I taken a class on how to talk to people. Never had I taken a class on how to listen to people. Nor had I ever taken a class on the art of asking questions and digging for deeper meaning behind the words. I had been satisfied with just moving through life, hopefully doing at least average in my life skills. I had a sense of humor, I had friends and I could preach. It wasn't that I didn't want to learn new skills. I simply was not aware that these were skills to develop. I didn't know what I didn't know.

At the same time I was taking mediation training, a good friend sat with me one time and asked, "How would you and Gwen like to attend the *Choices* program?" I had heard a few things about *Choices*, but I did not know much of what it was about. I just knew it was a place of personal growth, a life-skills workshop. We were interested in counseling, talking, and learning, so we were also open to discovering what *Choices* had to offer to us. I said, "I would love to go, but we could not financially afford that right now."

He asked, "What if that was taken care of for you?" And he quickly added, "Don't worry about paying me back. When you are financially able, just pay someone else's way for *Choices*. Just pay it forward."

I was amazed at his interest in us, and obviously his appreciation for the program. That's how we ended up at *Choices* in November of 2000, just seven months into the wilderness journey. I was already learning things in mediation training I had never thought of before, but I had no idea I was about to strap myself into a rocket ship of learning experiences.

I was totally unaware of how much I did not know about some life skills that I had just taken for granted. We never arrive at the graduation day of life itself. We can get certificates and degrees for high school, college, grad school, seminary, and a host of other things. We put the document in a frame and hang it on the wall. But graduation and diplomas are not the end, they are just the beginning. Now we must use that knowledge to enhance everyday life, or it's all just a waste of time.

But often, the classes we take for a degree don't help us when it comes to conflict, forgiveness, accountability, and apology. We also need to have the ability to get along with our neighbor, co-worker, or family member. We need to learn how to have peace within ourselves. There are so many things to learn. And I enjoyed the discovery of how much there was to learn.

At *Choices,* as well as through numerous other learning opportunities, I have become aware that it pays off to enter each day with curiosity. The list of insights I discovered seems endless, but a few highlights are accountability, self-defeating behavior, self-care, how to have more fun, the power of good questions, pretending, and being kind to myself. Maybe they would be of help to you too.

Accountability is the learning point that has anchored most everything else on my journey. Accountability for myself and for the decisions I have made and continue to make in life is the ultimate beginning point for everything else that comes after. While some things are out of my control, most challenges in life are simply about the decisions I make and my responses in the moment when I am confronted with events that I didn't choose or have no control over. We only have one life. I am accountable for every decision I make. No one "makes me" choose what I choose to do with the circumstances I face. This is not a dress rehearsal for a second turn at life, so I must own my life and take responsibility for how it is going right now. There was a lot of peace in coming to terms with and acknowledging that fact.

Blame is the opposite of accountability. So many people spend their lives looking for someone to criticize for everything that goes wrong for them. They experience life as a journey in "victimhood!" Many excuses are offered. "I can't overcome my situation because......" or "If it wasn't for you I would . . .", "If you understood my childhood. . ." Then, all the unfair events in life and in the world are easily listed. There were many ways I could have been much more accountable for the life I had lived than I had been willing to admit.

I was amazed to discover the number of ways I sabotage my own life and relationships. I was able to identify some of my own self-defeating behaviors. Procrastination, blame, criticism, broken agreements, the need to be right, my desire to control things that are not mine to control, and displaying a chippy or cynical attitude are just a few of the popular ones that I could identify with. They are self-defeating because even though we participate, our actions don't get us what we want out of life. Admitting my own personal self-defeating behaviors to myself actually brought a new awareness of how to live more successfully each day. It is also another layer of accountability.

I have become much more aware of how crucial it is to manage my time and my health, as well as my emotional balance and strength. For that to happen, I realize how important it is to say "no" sometimes to invitations or opportunities that come to me. They may be for things that I really want to do and would enjoy, but in order to not box myself in, I must decline. Space, rest, and slowing down are all ways to take care of ourselves so that we will have the energy to do the things we really need to do. It could be seen as selfish, but here is why it is not.

When we take care of ourselves, we have what we need in the reserve tank to take care of others. When we use up that reserve tank by a frenzied schedule, chasing objects and goals that keep us going flat out, we tend to then be exhausted and often make unwise decisions. I didn't realize how much it cost me and the important people in my life when I simply moved at the chaotic pace that life sometimes takes. More thought and discernment regarding what I can and can't take on is so refreshing. Taking care of our hearts, time and energy makes it possible to be better people in the world for everyone else too. The Bible has a wise verse. "Keep your heart with all vigilance, for from it flow the springs of life. Proverbs 4:23. It is never selfish to take care of ourselves.

I discovered that I had lost the playfulness of the child that I had been so many years ago. The carefree little boy named "Billy" was buried in the drama of my adult life and with the burdens of making a living and rebuilding my soul. Life was, in many ways, just too heavy. My child-like spirit may not have been dead, but it was on life-support. My mind was burdened with my regrets and there was no time or energy to just play, have fun and laugh, out loud! Play is not only necessary in order to have some fun, it is also energizing.

At two different retreats I attended, we did a scavenger hunt that involved some crazy, fun interaction with people. Asking for pictures with total strangers for a variety of reasons. Interacting with a police officer to explain that we needed her to write a parking ticket and then mark it void. It was against her regulations, but seeing the fun we were having she did it anyway. I was able to laugh like a child as we shared stories about how it went for other groups. I was being brought back to life with a child-like spirit to help tackle the heavy realities of life. It was much easier to go on in that frame of mind. We would all benefit if we would uncover the spontaneity of that child that has been buried somewhere in the past. I didn't know that, but I'm sure glad I found out.

Good questions, asked in the right way, can be life changing. I have shared some examples in these pages. I read in the book, *Fierce Conversations*, by Susan Scott, that if we are talking, we should be asking questions. That's the way we learn and can find out about others. It's the way we reach successful conclusions and change can begin.

I've heard more than one version of the story of the parent who asked his children after school each day, "Did you ask any good questions today?" The children decided that in order to have a good answer for their parents, they needed to start asking good questions. Because of that push, they excelled in their education, as well as in life.

Good questions get to the heart of the matter. They help us search for deep truth, not just answers. Many find what they believe to be the truth and are satisfied to leave it at that without exploring further to see if there is something else that could expand or deepen what they have just discovered. Like searching for treasure, there is an incredible opportunity awaiting us if we don't ever stop being curious about "what else" is possible.

It is important to ask good questions of others, of the books I read, or the internet sites I use for information. It's important to be careful without being critical. The questions I ask of others can help them learn as well, for when one pauses to reflect, new learning will often take place.

It is even more important to ask good questions of myself. That is the path to authenticity. When I am willing to interrogate my own thought patterns and processes, I may discover that I avoid certain things. By stepping over issues that I need to address, I'm simply avoiding the truth. Asking and answering good questions can be totally life-changing.

One good question I have learned to check in with myself is, "What am I pretending not to know?" I often ask that question of others, too. The answer, if we are willing to be honest, may uncover deep things that need to be dealt with that we are actually choosing to avoid. It may make the next steps in life hard and require the need to make deep change, but pretending everything is okay when we know it is not is never a solid ground on which to base any foundation for moving forward.

People may believe that the relationship they are in is fine and healthy, but when asked that question, they may pause, reflect and admit that they really are lonely and unhappy. When they stop to reflect, they admit they are just pretending that everything is fine. I'm not suggesting that the question is the door to breaking off all relationships, but it may be the door to doing something about changing and strengthening it.

I realized that I could keep living my life as I had known it, or I could apply the new skills I was learning and make some significant changes that would have a positive impact every day for the rest of my life. It was a choice that I could only make for me, and one that I could not make for anyone else. Each one is responsible for their own life. I thought back to how often I had wanted to take on the responsibility for others making good choices, and how foolish and futile that really was. I can hardly take responsibility for myself, let alone others. How refreshing it was to come to terms with the truth that I was not in charge of the world, and the people in it, after all!

I am now much more aware of how things from our childhood can impact every day in our adult experience if we let it. A child hearing from their parents that they "should do better" at school, chores, cleaning or any other task, may spend their whole lives believing they have to always do better. They spend their lives working to impress their parents, bosses, spouses and children. That often shifts into the belief that anything they do is not, and never will be, good enough. It becomes a never-ending treadmill. How freeing it is to realize that giving our best is, all by itself, actually good enough, and we can rest peacefully on that thought alone.

I remember one time telling myself not to turn on to a certain street because it would mean having to navigate several one-way streets to get to where I was going. As I was thinking that all through, I took the very turn I was reminding myself not to take. I laughed out loud and said to myself, "You are so stupid!" Then I immediately caught myself and added, "No, you aren't stupid, you just didn't do it the way you wanted to." We would do well to stop being so hard on ourselves.

The way we talk to ourselves and treat ourselves is despicable sometimes. A good question to breathe some air into our souls is to ask, "Would we allow others to treat or talk to a friend the way I treat or talk to myself?" If the answer is "Absolutely not!", then why is it okay for us to treat ourselves that way?

It was in 2005 and 2006 that I completed Life Coach training from *Coaches Training International.* This was an amazing opportunity to be exposed to ideas I had never known anything about before. I learned that we process our lives through different perspectives and stories. We view the memories about our lives as "the truth" and then live from our belief in that story.

An extension of the Life Coach training was a four-retreat Leadership training opportunity that was available. That was when I experienced the power of working through my fears through the high ropes work we did. It was here where I discovered how to lead from my own heart, but also how to lead with the energy of others. I found the value of silence as we spent 24 hours together without speaking or reading. We were only to be with our thoughts.

At one of the retreats, we did an exercise where I was amazed at the power that comes from asking for help. I have developed a mantra from that learning moment that "Strong people ask for help." There is such strength in the empowerment of using my own voice to clearly ask for what I want. I'm not suggesting that we stamp our foot and demand, but sometimes we don't clearly articulate what it is we are asking for and just assume the other will know what we mean.

At another point in this training, we were instructed to stand in front of the group and speak about anything on our minds for one minute. We didn't even have to make sense, just talk. Then we were to stay standing and graciously receive and accept the gift of the cheering, clapping, whistling and the raucous appreciation from others. We were not to sit or move, just stand and receive. It taught me the gift we give others when we allow them to offer their verbal or tangible gifts to us.

There were so many wonderful "lightbulb" moments in my journey. I just simply didn't know what I didn't know. The list is endless.

Some of these ideas are spelled out in detail in other chapters. I am writing this to challenge myself, and you, to watch for and participate in new learning opportunities, for the fresh awareness and insight it brings. I didn't know that I didn't know these things. I would have never learned them if I had not signed up for these many and varied learning events.

I don't remember ever saying, "I don't need to learn any more. I'm done learning." However, I have often been amazed at the awakening moments I have had in times that I least expected them to appear. I have another mantra that says, "I want to be learning when I die, and I want to slide into my grave sideways." I want to be busy learning until my last breath, not at some point becoming resigned to the fact that "I'm done learning. Now I'm just waiting to die."

You can't tell me what you don't yet know, and I can't tell you what I don't yet know. But we can all commit ourselves to learning something new each and every day. "Aha" moments happen when we least expect them to appear.

God is the master teacher. There is much to be learned in the wilderness. It's often a place where God can get our full attention. He takes us places we don't necessarily plan to go, but He has a reason for it. He has wisdom He wants us to learn. The Bible is a lesson book all on its own, with lessons for this life as well as lessons to prepare for an eternal life of no negativity or death. Who knows what we have yet to learn about getting ready for that life?

The Bible has a book called Proverbs, which is a book of many wise principles that have eternal value to them. One of them says this, "Pay attention to my wisdom; listen carefully to my wise counsel. Then you will learn to be discreet and will store up knowledge." Proverbs 5:1 (NLT)

There are 31 chapters in that book to teach us values that will carry us through the days of our existence. How can we know them unless we read them? We don't know what we don't know, but as we turn the pages of that Book and through the events of life, may we all continue to be amazed at what is out there for us. And may we never decide we have learned enough, and we are done!

LESSONS LEARNED

1. Finding someone to blame, criticize or condemn when things go wrong never creates community or friendship. Being accountable for my life, my decisions, and my part when things don't go right is a sign of responsibility and strength.

2. I must be open to any opportunity that comes. There may be gold nuggets of truth in the most unexpected places.

3. There is value if we approach life with an attitude that has a curious edge to it. Every day. Live in the wonder of what this day and the people we will meet holds for us and our learning.

4. Never be content to say, "I've learned enough. I'm done."

COMPASS POINTS

1. How common is the attitude of "accountability" in your everyday life and activities? Explain.

2. What would change for you if you intentionally stepped into new learning opportunities just to find out something you don't already know?

3. What learning goals could you set for yourself? Could you sign up for a new class? Set a reading goal, and read books from a variety of topics? Are there others you can list?

4. What are the truths in your life that you are "pretending not to know?" Where in your life do you need to make changes? What is stopping you from making those changes?

There is a part of us that craves someone
in our lives to provide safety and calm strength. Especially
when we are vulnerable, afraid, and alone.

From the Wilderness

Creating a safe place for people to share their words, fears
and hopes is one of the best gifts we can give
to another human.

From the Wilderness

8

I JUST WANT TO BE HEARD

The cry of the human heart is for connection. Babies of any species feel safest with the mother or father present. Troubled children find calm and peace when they are held, cuddled, and nurtured. We were designed that way by a Creator who built love into our DNA.

We all want to be known by at least one other person. More would be great, but if we have at least one, it's a good thing. We want to be known by more than our name and hobbies and favorite color or sports team. We all want to be known from deep within by someone. At least one. There is a part of us that craves someone in our lives to provide safety and calm strength. Especially when we are vulnerable, afraid, and alone.

Through my journey I have found that the word "safety" is becoming more and more important. I have experienced it myself and I hear the heart cry of others so often for that very deep need.

In my work as a mediator, I have worked with hundreds of couples who need to make parenting plans regarding their children. The moms and dads are not together anymore for a variety of reasons. It's not my job to counsel them on reconciliation, some are already remarried and living new stories. I am there to mediate a discussion and to determine what they can agree on for the purpose of providing good parenting for the children. It's not only the parents who are working through these changes. It impacts the entire family.

I often draw a picture for the parents. I put their names on the paper and draw a line to connect them. I explain that this line represents the relationship they had before there were any children. They could call it whatever they want. Friends. Lovers. Soulmates. Whatever would best describe it. Couples do not connect at first in a place of anger or conflict.

Then children arrive and I draw two lines down to a meeting point and put a "C" at the bottom to represent that. Half-way down those lines I write Dad and Mom. Then I draw a line across between "mom" and "dad" and tell them this line represents your parenting relationship.

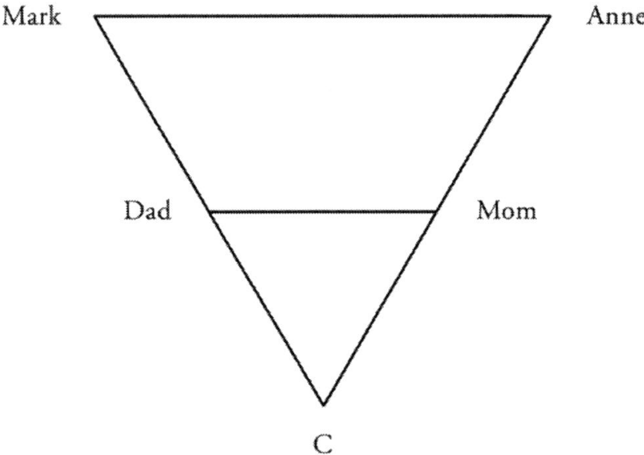

At that time, I put a series of "X"s across the top line and explain that this relationship has changed. I remind them the reason they are meeting with me is that we are searching for ways to make the parenting relationship as strong as possible for the sake of their children. I remind them that they are the only front-line team these children have who will meet their needs as they grow to maturity.

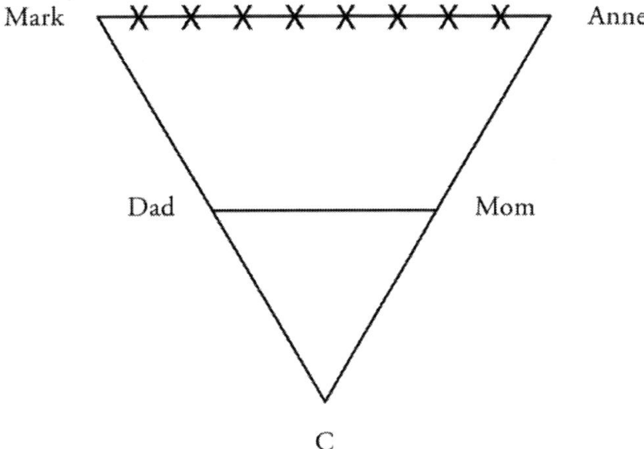

I also explain that sometimes parents have a lot of leftover emotional pain from the relationship line, and they want to continue the fight over the issues that drove them apart. For those parents, since the relationship is broken, if they have unresolved tension and conflict, the only area they have left to argue in is regarding the needs of the children. That is the only relationship that still connects them. Since the relationship line has changed and they don't have that connection anymore, they bring the conflict down to that parenting line, and the children are left without a team. Some simply choose to do a lot of that. I have sadly watched parents use their children as pawns as they seek revenge or control over each other.

I appeal to them that it would be life-changing for their children if they could "lay their swords down," leave them in my office and determine to be a strong team for the sake of their children. I remind them that they don't have to be lovers, or even like each other, but it would be very helpful for the children if they could be polite, respect each other, and work together to meet the children's needs.

I heard about a young man who grew up in an environment where, if his parents ever crossed paths, there was generally a dramatic scene of some kind, complete with harsh, loud words. The boy didn't ever want to be with his mom and dad at the same time.

When he was finishing his grade twelve year, his high school principal came to him and said, "Here are your two tickets to invite people to graduation. However, I am asking you to invite either your mom or your dad, but not both. We do not want to have something happen to upset the program." The boy understood completely and invited his grandparents. Neither parent was invited. I find that story heartbreaking.

The good news is that I often meet with parents who are absolutely committed to parenting their children in healthy, supportive ways. They will sell houses and move to the same city where the children live, even the same street or neighborhood, so that the children can easily be with either parent. Often these children are given freedom to visit with mom or dad whenever the schedule will allow. These parents work to give their children a safe and happy environment where they can freely talk about mom to dad, and about dad to mom, without fear of a conflict as a result. It's all about safety, and good parents commit themselves to work hard to create a safe space for their children.

Parents who work like that for their children, hear and respond to a deep calling. They want their parenting to not hurt their children, despite the fact the relationship between the two of them as lovers or friends seems to be beyond repair.

I often suggest to moms and dads that if their children were to ever write a biography one day, the material for that book is being given to them right now, in the way they as their parents work as a team, or not, for the children. Then I ask, "Do you want them to write about how bitter their parents were, and how that played out in their lives? Or do you want them to write about how their parents were amazing in spite of the fact that they couldn't be in a personal relationship with each other?"

The reason I have shared all of this is because it has given me an insight into the human craving for connection. People just want to be heard. Not merely their words, but they also want to be heard from their heart. Deep change happens when we learn to listen for the cry of the heart behind the words.

Sometimes parents argue very strongly over the simplest things. For example, one time I was working with parents who were arguing over the cost of travel for the parents to have regular visits with the child. It boiled down to a heated discussion over the amount of $42.

In another case, the argument became very heated over whether they should swap the car seat between the parents' vehicles whenever they exchanged visiting time with the child, or whether they should spend the money to buy a second car seat and have one in each vehicle. They each wanted it a different way.

Another couple became quite heated over what amount the child support payments should be, and they reached an angry impasse over a $50 discrepancy.

In all three of these situations, I asked the same question. "It's my guess that this is not the real issue. What is it that you are really arguing about?" The answer was always some version of the same basic human need. "You are correct. That is not the real issue. The real issue is that I have not been heard or respected for ages and I'm finally standing up for something. I'm not backing down on this one."

I'm sure you can recognize that it's not just parenting relationships where people do not feel heard. Friends, spouses, lovers, and work colleagues all have the same need.

I know of couples where one just needs to share their fear and be acknowledged for the simple fact that they *are* afraid. The partner doesn't want to give any space to the fear because it is thought that the fear might grow bigger, so they point out all the logical reasons the fear is unfounded. When the one needing a soft ear does not receive it, the relationship becomes stuck and is simply treading water. Tolerance may allow the relationship to continue, but the loss of closeness and intimacy is very real.

Even though I experience this frequently in my work and I see it played out with many people, I still fall into the trap personally from time to time. I remember having a discussion one day with Gwen about a concern we had discussed many times on how to support someone that we both knew and loved. We did not have any answers for the situation, no matter how many times we had discussed it before. She brought it up again and I was not in a mood to talk it all through even one more time. I had no more answers than I had before. So, I put my hand up to send the very clear, "Stop! I don't want to talk about this again", message. It was very rude, and hurtful. I well remember the look on her face.

I immediately recognized what I had done, and I apologized. The fact that I didn't have any answers did not negate the fact that she needed to be heard for the burden she carried about the situation. We do not have to have all the answers, but we can still stop and listen with deep care and attention.

Employers who want to nurture their employees, as well as receive an honest day's work from them, realize that providing a safe environment for feedback or questions will pay rich dividends. When the people who carry the production workload do not feel they have a safe place to talk to leadership, where they can share concerns they might have, they will no doubt talk amongst themselves. This alone can really have a negative effect on the morale and atmosphere of the work environment. A good place to work requires both management and employees to have a way to ensure the safety of expression whenever one needs to be heard.

At the time of this writing, the whole world is locked into the confusion around the Covid-19 pandemic. Parts of the world are in government-imposed lockdown. Some are in recommended lockdown. Vaccine use and distribution are hot topics of discussion. And the viability and need to wear masks has people divided and adamant on both sides of the issue.

The disagreement comes at many levels. Some are very quiet, but no doubt have opinions that are very real. Others are extremely vocal through whatever platform they can find and are not afraid to speak out. And then, some go to the extreme and judge, accuse and even threaten others who do not see it their way.

To me, it is a sad thing that we cannot disagree and yet still respect those who share different opinions. Good listening skills do not mean we will always agree. It simply means we will always create a safe place for people to share their deepest thoughts, emotions and opinions whether there is agreement or not. Others have come to the conclusions they have by whatever route it took them to arrive there. We don't have to reject people just because we disagree with them. We can always listen.

If the relationship matters, the bottom line of all disagreement is that each position must be heard and respected as personal and legitimate to that person. People just want to be heard.

If we are not satisfied until we have convinced everyone else to come to our position, we face a lifelong struggle. "I'm right," is one of the most destructive self-defeating behaviors we can engage in. This takes us to a place of insisting on being right instead of creating or allowing a safe place to disagree. We do not provide a listening spirit if our goal is only to convince others to come to our way of thinking. How much happier the world would be if we listened to each other without judgment and offered them the respect that we would cherish for ourselves. Some just live their lives more determined to be right than happy.

Too many people experience a lot of pain and hurt in life. Sometimes it is from the very people we believe we should be able to trust the most. All people at some point in their lives will need a safe place to talk and be heard. Even just one person, who will listen with their heart as much as their ears. I meet people regularly who are angry at another, many times simply because they just have not been given the listening ear they so craved and deserved. It's not self-pity or selfish. It's simply a genuine need of the human heart.

As I have worked through the many layers of healing and growth from my own life journey, I have been so blessed with people who have taken time to go deep with me and hear not just my words, but my heart as well. As I watch it play out before my eyes with people I work with, I often simply detect the unspoken cry that says, "I just want to be heard."

When people shout and raise their voices at each other, it's a signal that they are not feeling listened to. When one does not feel heard it's a common response to raise the decibel level of our voices because we think if we speak louder, then for sure the other person will listen. The reality is that people are hearing the words. Volume is not the issue. The listener is just not hearing the heart or the message behind the words, and a louder volume will make no difference.

I've experimented with this. When I have people in my mediation office and one of them begins to raise their voice as they talk, I tune in to the fact that they just want to be listened to. I'll ask them, "I am thinking you are not feeling heard. Would that be correct?" They often acknowledge that to be true. I'll go on to say in a quiet voice, "So we are going to listen very carefully. What exactly is it that you would like us to hear?"

It's always amazing to me what happens next. The person gets a much quieter and softer tone of voice and begins to talk. They choose their words carefully and do their best to be clear. When they know they are being listened to, there is no need for volume or anger. We all just want to be heard.

I have been so blessed with so many friends who have crossed my path that have learned the skill of listening. They have been invaluable, and we have rejoiced and laughed together as my soul was being restored. I have had life coaches who have asked deep questions for me to think over and have really cared to hear my answers. Then, they have probed my answers to make sure I was not avoiding my own heart truth. It's been such a gift. I, in turn, want to return that favor to others.

Blended with that is the desire to be the kind of person who can create a safe place so that people feel safe to talk. Providing a safe place for people to share their words, fears and hopes is one of the best gifts that we can give to another human. Friend or new acquaintance, it makes no difference. Talking to a stranger on an airplane has the same possibility. Without having ever met them before, I already know that they want to be heard and seen. It's a natural heart cry.

On three different occasions, I was invited to speak to an assembly of pastors and share a bit of my heart story through the dark days and into recovery and healing. It was not easy, but it was always rewarding. We are humans with weakness and frailty. To stand in front of a group of colleagues and talk about weakness and failure is very hard. But what happened each time was very interesting. Without fail, a few people would come to me afterwards with tears in their eyes just to talk to me. They just wanted to talk to someone about the pain in their own lives that they had never felt safe to share with anyone. They just wanted to be heard and believed that because I had openly shared my heart with them, they had finally met someone who they trusted would understand because there were similarities that they could relate to. The reality is that we don't connect with others in our strengths very well, but we certainly bond in our shared brokenness and vulnerability.

I have learned much about understanding the need to listen and allow people to talk. But the very best part is that I have learned that

God also wants to listen. He has not closed Himself to anyone. He is not the tyrant some have made Him to be. The Bible story basically demonstrates how God says, "I see you. I know everything about you. I love you. Come, let's talk." He is not shocked by our mistakes. He does not keep track of our mistakes. He does not have a limit to the number of mistakes He will forgive and then cut off His grace. He loves to hear us and create a safe environment for us to be vulnerable toward Him. He listens and loves, regardless of whatever road one might have traveled and the stories we must talk to Him about.

He knows us and He loves us. I want to talk to anyone who believes they have committed too many mistakes or sins for God to still love them. God cannot stop loving us. He simply is not able to stop. The only thing He cannot do is force us to accept His love and start loving Him in return. That is always a free choice and loving Him will remain voluntary on our part. If you have bought into the picture that God's love has a limit, I urge you to dig a little deeper into the story about Him. Meet Him again as if for the first time. Read the story as a child taking in every word. His love is deeper than any ill-fated choices or mistakes one might ever make.

He wants us to know that if we cannot find another human to hear us, He will hear us. We cannot surprise Him, and He cannot turn us away. He never ignores a hurting heart, and He never says "Sorry, last month I was ready to forgive you, but you have gone too far now." Jesus said when He was here, "those the Father has given me will come to me, and I will never reject them." John 6:37 (NLT) When Jesus says "never reject", He truly does mean never.

We are blessed when we have a spouse to deeply listen to us. We are blessed to have parents we can talk to, or children who take in what we say. Friends that give us room to be heard are a gift like no other. And best of all there is a God who says, "I know you want to be heard. Let's talk."

LESSONS LEARNED

1. The human heart craves a listening ear. I need one, and I can learn to provide a safe environment for a friend who is looking for someone to talk to.

2. We give the greatest gift when we open doors for people to feel welcome and safe to deeply share their heart with us.

3. There is a God who listens better than any of us and knows our every need. He will never ever turn us away.

4. Listening for the heart, more than words, moves us to much deeper places in all our relationships.

COMPASS POINTS

1. Who in your life is the one or the ones who listen to you best?

2. Who in your life comes to you because they know that they will always have a safe, listening ear?

3. What might you do differently to assure that you are a safe and deep listener of people's hearts?

I JUST WANT TO BE HEARD

NOTES FOR MY BACKPACK

The desire to fail forward would mean to stop hoping to have a better past and instead stay committed to creating a future I could be proud of.

From the Wilderness

Failure should be our teacher, not our undertaker. It is delay, not defeat. It is a temporary detour, not a dead-end street.

William A. Ward

9

FINISH WELL

Kelly Clarkson's popular song, *What Doesn't Kill You Makes You Stronger*, sums up a great deal of my wilderness journey. She passionately belts out that what doesn't kill us makes taller, and stronger fighters in life. I was introduced to the song when the nurses on my daughter's hospital unit made a video of young cancer patients lip syncing to the song. It was very powerful to hear it in that setting of hurting and weakened bodies. While the song is talking about overcoming a broken relationship, I resonated with the message and heard it from the context of a broken life.

When my life changed and I entered this wilderness, it was devastating. Behind me was a life that was precious and rewarding. It was all I had known. I had trained for nothing else, and I had never, ever thought about changing. I had no alternatives to turn to or fall back on. Ahead of me was a completely blank page. The future was bleak, empty, barren and foreboding. Recently, I saw part of the old 1956 movie, *The Ten Commandments.* I watched the part when Moses, (Charlton Heston) left Egypt, the life he had known, and headed off into the wilderness. It was hot, deserted, and lonely. I could relate on so many levels. It was a great visual for me in the context of writing this book.

I thought back to my memories of those first days of entering the wilderness in April of 2000. As dark as I felt, I never once thought of taking my own life. However, I clearly remember thinking that I could understand why, for some, it would be a choice they would consider, or even act upon. I could understand why one might choose to just drive off a cliff rather than face the questions, harsh judgment, gossip, and the long, unknown road. As tough as that moment was for me, I forced myself to think beyond that moment to better times. I just didn't know when those better times would come and what it would take to get there.

I am a fan of John Maxwell, the pastor and author of many books on leadership and teamwork. In his book, *Failing Forward,* he speaks about the differences between failing backward and failing forward.

He suggests that we fail backward when we blame others, repeat the same mistakes, expect to continually fail, decide that we are failures, stay stuck in past mistakes, and quit altogether. As I read his book, I could really see the futility in adopting any one of those attitudes.

He goes on to suggest that when we fail forward, we work to be accountable, learn from our mistakes, accept that failure is a part of progress, maintain a positive attitude and move forward with perseverance.

From my first step into the wilderness, I decided that however faltering those steps might be, I was not going to become an isolated hermit. I was going to rebuild my life to something that could yet be useful. I didn't want to be remembered as a disappointment and a failure when I died.

I was invited to consider a work opportunity that was hundreds of miles away from where I lived in Red Deer, Alberta, Canada. It was tempting. The thought of beginning life again in a new environment where I was not known would be much easier in some ways. Having to face people and friends on a regular basis who tried to figure out what to say when they saw me was awkward for all of us. How sweet it would be to just get up, go to work and not have reminders of my past around me all the time.

In the end, the opportunity never materialized, and I'm glad it did not. As appealing as many things might have been, there was another side to that coin. Running away had benefits. Staying also had benefits. We were living in an area close to where we had attended high school and college, so we had many friends and had family there as well. Even if we did move away, we would for sure come back for visits on a regular basis. I pictured it like this. If we moved and then came back to visit family and friends or for a school event, alumni gathering, or church camp program, we would be just as awkward then as we would be if we just stayed and faced people now. Why not step up, be visible and get it behind us, rather than have to do it later anyway.

It was not easy, and it took a while to start to relax around people. I could easily make up stories about how they must be talking about me. My mind worked overtime, whether it was true or not. Each opportunity to be in the presence of friends and acquaintances made it a little easier to do again. Each faltering step produced a little more courage to take the next one. With the help of Gwen, who stood by my side and appeared in places with me, it became easier and sweeter. Hiding would have been failing backward. Facing life with determination was making me stronger.

A buddy of mine has often repeated, "I've given up all hope of having a better past." How easy it would be to lay awake at night beating myself up with my regrets. How I wanted to beg God to turn back time. Neither of those would work or change anything about the reality I was facing. The desire to fail forward would mean to stop hoping to have a better past and instead stay committed to creating a future that I could be proud of.

When I was taking life coach training, we did an exercise called Future Self. We were asked to close our eyes and imagine a scenario where we would be transported off the Earth for a period of twenty years and then to return to the changed Earth that we would find. We were to imagine ourselves walking up to the door of a house, knocking on the door, knowing that we were about to meet the version of ourselves with twenty more years of time and experience.

We were to quietly observe that version of ourselves that we saw and notice what we were drawn to and what we were proud of. We were to have an imaginary conversation with that person and ask them for advice for the next twenty years.

When I was a boy, I had imaginary friends who I spoke to as they "played with me" in my yard. It was easy and it was fun entertainment for me. As an adult, I'm not prone to imagine and make stuff up, but I really enjoyed the visuals of this exercise. In my imagination, the man who came to the door to greet me was a gentleman who I would love to meet anywhere, and I was excited to spend some time with him. I didn't want to leave. He made me comfortable and had good advice for me.

What I took away from that exercise was that if I continued to act in a respectable and honorable way, I would one day be that person. If I was kind to people, forgave people, respected people, the same would be given back to me in return. If I were to live with the integrity and values that truly mattered to me, I would become the man in that exercise. I could stay stuck trying to create a better past, or I could act in ways that would make that man I visualized come to life. That would be failing forward.

I am a self-proclaimed, hopeless optimist. No matter what happens, I tend to look for the bright side and grasp on to the fact that I will work through the current situation and come out winning on the other side. Maintaining a positive attitude has been a gift that I have enjoyed my whole life. I am fully aware that it is not so easy for others and that makes me sad. By having an upbeat approach to life, I never gave up hope that I would find meaning in the wilderness I was entering. I was determined to find opportunities and places where there would be refreshing shade and water as opposed to the dry, dusty desert. This was not going to kill me. I was committed to the belief that this journey was going to build me into a better person.

I guess that's why Kelly Clarkson's song spoke to me. I could let my life and my failure destroy me, or I could use it as a steppingstone to the future. I was determined to not let the wilderness kill me and to be a strong fighter as the dust settled around me. My use of the word "fighter" simply means to never give up. I wasn't going to let what I was going through destroy me but instead resolved to let it make me stronger, stand taller, and keep persevering through it all, and finish well, no matter what.

I do not define success as position, money, bank account or fame. Success is getting up again after falling, even with dirt on my face, wiping it off, and creating a future. It is being able to look God in the eye and acknowledge my failure and my need for Him. And it doesn't matter to me if anyone else on the planet notices or applauds. It only matters that I can step ahead with the smile of God on my shoulder. I didn't see Him smiling at my failure, but I did see Him smile when I looked at Him and wanted to create a future with Him. That was enough.

I'm not here to pat myself on the back. I don't know how to measure whether I've failed forward or not. I could not settle to just stay down or stuck. I want to grow from the lessons in my life. There is no point in learning if we don't apply what we have learned. I want anyone who can learn from my life to take any of these lessons and apply it to themselves. I created a purpose statement for my life while I attended the *Choices* Seminar. It is that I want to live my life "encouraging others to finish well." I have come to believe that no matter the road that got us to where we are, we always have the choice to "finish well."

It is my commitment to myself to finish well. My wilderness journey has not killed me, and I can see now with 21 years of life experience since then, that God and life have made me stronger. I am stronger in my determination to live an accountable, transparent and honorable life. One wilderness journey is enough in a lifetime.

I am stronger in the way I talk and relate to my wife, family, and friends. I look for and enjoy deeper conversations about the things that really matter. I'm not hiding secrets, so I don't have to be careful about what I say. I want my life to be an open book. It makes it much easier to just enjoy life in the moment.

I experience a more satisfying walk with God. We can talk easily, and I know that He never, ever was angry, just very sad. His only fear was that I might not turn my face fully back to His. He is a loving and forgiving Friend. He knows my heart and loves me despite my humanity. He knows the frailty of the human heart and spirit, which is why He made dramatic plans to rescue us. His work is to save and not condemn. He knows that humans condemn each other far too much, but that is not His way of treating us.

I have a much deeper appreciation and gentleness toward others who have made poor choices. I get it, I've been there. People don't wake up and decide to sabotage their lives. We don't live in a vacuum. I understand that and I have a deep sense of empathy for people who struggle with regret. I want to do all I can in the service of others to encourage them that no matter where their journey has taken them, there is always a way to find their way home and finish well. Someday, when I need a tombstone, I would like it to simply say, "He Finished Well."

LESSONS LEARNED

1. Failure brings options. We get to choose if we will fail backward or fail forward.

2. Adding failure to failure makes no sense. It was an opportunity to find beauty from ashes and see what could be salvaged.

3. Success is not things or positions, it's an inside job. It's a commitment to finishing well no matter where life has taken us.

COMPASS POINTS

1. When you fail are you more likely to fail backward or fail forward?

2. What failure or regret still holds you hostage to your memory and your past?

3. What steps will you take to let go and embrace a determined commitment to finish well?

NOTES FOR MY BACKPACK

Secrets hold dark power over our lives,
but light always dispels darkness.

From the Wilderness

A man who can keep a secret may be wise,
but he is not half as wise as
the man with no secrets to keep.

E. W. Howe

10

SECRETS KEEP US SICK

A Proverb in the Bible says "A merry heart does good, like medicine. But a broken spirit dries the bones." Proverbs 17:22 NKJV

Nothing breaks the spirit like keeping a secret. Not the secret from a friend which should always be kept sacred. I'm speaking about the secret of a dark truth that is hidden deep in the heart. The secret life, being lived contrary to one's value system, causing them to portray a false front to others. The secret that one guards with every ounce of energy they have, determined that no one else can ever find out.

The sad truth is that for a period of time my life was a false front. I was one person to my family and friends, and I was another person to myself. To others, I was the person I truly wanted to be. To myself, I was living in a secret world, stumbling along outside my value system. I was not proud of that, and I was not at peace. The fear of the expected consequences should my secret be revealed, overshadowed my integrity. I was fearful of the result of where transparency and truth would take me. I should have just done the right thing and faced the wilderness, but I truly wanted to find a way to avoid the shame and fallout that would surely follow. Avoidance is a picture of human nature in all its glory, but human nature is never glorious. I am not proud of that chapter in my life story but neither do I make excuses or defend myself for the way I managed it.

My secret had taken over my life. I continually thought of others, "You can like the me that I present to you, but if I were to present to you the real me, you would probably reject me." The real me went into hiding. Hiding creates darkness, and darkness wears on the soul. My soul was crushed, but I didn't want anyone to know it, nor did I want anyone to ever find out.

I came to experience the truth that secrets are every bit as confining as prisons, bars and chains. I could fully relate to David in the Bible who said, "When I refused to confess my sin, I was weak and miserable, and I groaned all day long. Day and night your hand of discipline was heavy on me. My strength evaporated like water in the summer heat." Psalm 32:3 (NLT)

Maybe there are times you have held on to a deep secret of some kind. Maybe you are holding one right now. Some carry secrets from something said or done even many years ago. I understand how hard that is. Secrets keep us sick. We tell ourselves that we can fix our situations alone, and by doing so simply isolate ourselves, and make it even harder to step out into the light, and into a place of strength and freedom.

Secrets are like a rock in the shoe. That little pebble is irritating at first, but as time goes on it becomes a source of festering pain under the blister that is caused. Like pebbles on the feet, secrets create blisters on the heart and there is no band aid big enough for that. Until the secret is actually addressed there is no relief, and there never will be.

I offer no advice for you on how you should deal with your secret circumstances should you be living in one. Each must walk their own journey, and while others may tell you what you should or should not do, it is ultimately between you and God. He will tell you, and it is best to follow whatever He says. If it means entering your own wilderness, I can testify that there are treasures and good lessons to be learned there. Hard times can also be very rich times.

For me, the power my secret held over me was broken when I sat to have the honest conversation with my wife that I should have had much earlier. I opened my story up to her and divulged the awful truth of my double life. I did not hide anything, and the poisoned dam was broken open as I spoke the truth of my secret life out loud. It was the hardest thing I've ever done. And yet, as hard as it was, it was in that same moment that a light turned on deep within me. Secrets hold dark power over our lives, but the light of the truth always dispels that darkness.

Should you ever get up in the dark of the night and open the fridge door, the darkness does not invade the fridge. The small light from the fridge invades the darkness. That's what happened to my soul when I began to speak the truth out loud. Although I faced the many and varied consequences of my secret becoming public knowledge, the freedom that came as a result, despite those consequences, was far greater than the prison my heart had been in.

Jesus said, "Whoever seeks to save his life will lose it, and whoever loses his life will preserve it." Luke 17:33, NKJV

The Scriptures don't lie and there is such truth in those words. Keeping the secret was my effort to save my life. It was my attempt to avoid consequences and embarrassment, even though I fully deserved the consequences and embarrassment. The hard work I put in to preserve my life as I knew it was an effort that had no merit or hope of realization. I exchanged that effort for my peace of mind and heart. When I lost my life as I had known it, I paid a big price, but at the same time I once again recovered the peace of mind and heart I had squandered.

Attached to the lesson of the destructive power of secrets is what I also learned about the power that honesty and forgiveness have in the ability to destroy that darkness. Exposing a secret is like unlocking the door to a prison, but the door doesn't open automatically. Freedom requires pushing that door open and walking through it. Where does one find the courage to walk out into the daylight?

As I spoke with Gwen and poured light into the darkness of my heart as I exposed the truth, I became more and more courageous. That night brought little sleep, and as we talked through the dark hours through to the light of day, a new life began to form within me. I was finally getting back in touch with the values that I had buried for so long. My soul was finally finding wind for its sails once again.

I found courage to continue talking, because while Gwen was devastated and in shock, she continued to listen. Her confusion exposed a full range of emotion, but there was room in those emotions to keep talking and sorting through the feelings that both she and I were experiencing. Through all of that, and the days and months that followed, I found the courage to walk out of the secret prison and stay in the daylight.

How does one keep from having dark secrets in the first place? Well, we all know that the answer to that question is pretty obvious. Never do anything or say anything that needs to be kept a secret in the first place. It's just that simple.

Of course, I'm not talking about the Christmas or birthday gift you have buried in the closet or the secret party or surprise visit from grandpa and grandma that you are planning. Those are the innocent secrets that bring pleasure. I'm talking about words and actions that you just don't want anyone else to know. If those are never done, dark secrets cannot form. It's really very simple and it's also very logical. It's the human heart, left to its own devising, that takes us places that lock up our hearts. If we guard our hearts and never do anything we are not proud of, we will never have to worry that a ringing phone is THAT phone call that might just come to shatter our lives.

And there is another whole side to keeping secrets. Secrets that lock up our souls in darkness need to be given the fresh air of honesty. However, somebody else's story that is not flattering to them in any way should always be kept a secret. It should not be shared by us for any reason.

I was at church one day, a few weeks after I had resigned from my pastoral career. I was happy to see a friend of ours from out of town, visiting that day with her mother. I went to speak with her and as we were chatting, I mentioned that I was not pastoring any more, assuming she would have heard the news about our recent events.

She looked surprised and asked, "Why not?"

I looked at her mother with the question in my eyes that said, "You didn't tell her?" She read my mind and simply responded with, "Some stories don't need to be repeated."

I was silent as I took in the gift that mother had given to me. She had not felt the need to share that scandalous story with her daughter who knew me and Gwen well. That was a secret she had simply stored away in her gracious heart. I found that very honoring to my bruised soul.

I have no idea who all talked and shared my failure with others. I heard some comments that had been made that told me people were talking. I was not surprised. I hold no grudges. We all battle with human nature. I have enough challenges to keep my own tongue under control, let alone worry about what others are saying.

A life of freedom is the payoff we receive for never having secrets that we must keep hidden.

LESSONS LEARNED

1. Dark secrets hold us hostage and keep us sick.

2. Freedom only comes when we become honest and deal with the truth in spite of the consequences.

3. The world is searching for people of integrity. If integrity has been compromised, it can be restored by truth, confession, and repentance.

4. We can help the secret-keeper by not judging or condemning them when we do hear it, which would only make them feel worse than they already do.

5. When we hear of the secrets of others that are not flattering, the story should stay locked in our heart. "Some stories don't need to be repeated."

COMPASS POINTS

1. Are there any secrets you are holding on to right now that are keeping you stuck in a dark place? If so, how long will you allow that secret to hold you hostage?

2. Are other people's secrets safe with you? Why or why not?

The cost of lowering the price of admission to the heart can be very high. Unfortunately, it often means the setting aside of morals and values that, in the end, sacrifice everyday peace and joy.

From the Wilderness

Discomfort is the price of admission to a meaningful life.

Susan David

11

THE PRICE OF ADMISSION

I'm wondering if you might have done what I sometimes do when it comes to spending money. I confess that I have paid more money for some things than the item was actually worth. Apparently, it was worth that much to me since I paid for it. We exchange money for items daily and we do it according to our own personal value system.

When we go to the store to buy groceries, clothes, books, or tools, we don't usually negotiate the price. We pay the sticker price and move on. When we buy a ticket for an entertainment or sports event, unless we buy the ticket from the street vendors, we order the ticket and pay the expected price. With many items, we look at the price and pay it because we want the item and are willing to pay whatever it takes to have it.

When it comes to bigger items like houses and automobiles, we feel more open to offer less than the asking price to see if we can get a better deal for the item of interest. And, sellers of big items are fully prepared to receive offers other than the posted price. Some people are known for their negotiation skills and buying things for much less than the asking price. It becomes a game and it's simply the thrill of the sport of wheeling and dealing. This is all about purchasing.

When we sell, we reverse the process. We want as much as possible for the item sold. Some are not concerned about market value. They simply want the highest price they can receive. They will argue and hold firm for the sake of a few dollars. Whenever there is an opportunity to make or lose money, it may reveal something about our character if we will look closely.

If all I want is the cheapest price and am willing to fight and argue for it, I might want to look at my willingness to put myself in the other person's shoes. What would I want if I was the seller? If all I want is the highest price on an item and am not willing to even sell the item until I get my price, I may want to consider why it might be better to at least have some monetary compensation for the item rather than still have the item in my hand at the end of the day.

The prices we are willing to pay and accept on every-day and tangible items may reveal something about our willingness to negotiate the deeper heart issues of life.

How much are you worth? How much is your heart or your soul worth? That part of you that makes up your integrity, character, and reputation. I can think of many people I have met and known along my journey who have negotiated with their value systems and integrity and have settled for far less than their dreams in life. At great cost to themselves. I am one of those people, and my wilderness journey began because of my lack of caution to guard the worth of my heart and soul. We just have a "knowing." We don't have to be told or reminded when we have strayed off course.

We were designed by a Creator who placed high values and integrity within us. We know when we have done something wrong. We have consciences that are moved and challenged by the actions we take.

The first murder recorded in the Bible was committed by a man named Cain who killed his brother, Abel. The story tells us that God asked Cain, "Where is your brother? Where is Abel?" Cain replied, "I don't know, am I my brother's guardian?" Genesis 4:9 (NLT) He knew he had done wrong but did not want to admit it. It was written on his conscience, which was speaking to him, and he did not want to listen.

People know that stealing, killing, lying and adultery are wrong. They know it deep inside, which is why they don't talk casually about it or openly admit it when something happens. The internal response we experience when we have gone against our conscience, reminds us that it was planted there by the Designer of life. He not only designed our bodies. He also designed and placed a conscience within each of us, complete with boundaries and reminders.

Human nature, being what it is, has become adept at negotiating the things of the heart, not just the price of an item for sale.

I can think of people of both genders who have searched for a safe and intimate relationship with someone they can love and trust. They knew what they were looking for and the ideals they had for their search. As they met people who had potential to be the partner they were looking for, they were excited about some things, and sometimes also disappointed in other things that became evident. Some determined that the price of admission to their heart was high and needed to stay high. They felt the need to end the relationship despite all the good things they could list. The price of admission was attached to the value they placed on their own heart and soul.

I recently read a poignant Facebook quote that said;

"Was it hard?" I ask.

"Letting go?"

I nodded.

"Not as hard as holding on to something that wasn't real."

I love the power of that. The price of admission to this person's heart was high, and their integrity gave them the power to end something that was asking too much.

I can think of others who, on the same search, decided that they would lower the price of admission and compromise some of the things that mattered to them in order to enjoy at least some type of connection and relationship. The relationship did not offer all that they were searching for, but it was not all bad either. There were some really good things present as well, and since there were some good things, the sticker price on the heart was lowered.

The cost of lowering the price of admission to the heart can be very high. Unfortunately, the cost usually involves the setting aside of morals and values that, in the end, sacrifice everyday peace and joy. People continue to go through life putting on a brave front and a happy smile, while inside they are confused and disappointed. I have watched in sadness as some have stayed in relationships with people who were destructive to their morals, joy, happiness, and peace. For reasons that only they know, they are willing to sell for a lowered price of admission.

I understand that sometimes the issues are complex, and I do not want to minimize anyone's experience. We hear the rare stories of people chained in dungeons, basements, closets, bedrooms and the like, who are threatened and treated like slaves or animals. We hear other stories of threats and fear placed upon individuals that leave them paralyzed, and they stay enslaved emotionally. The stories of human trafficking are beyond tragic, and I dare not even try to suggest that I can understand the prison these people are in. These are not the situations I am referring to. People in these type of situations are just hoping to survive.

I am thinking of those, who come and go with freedom and may have a fulfilling life in many ways, but who, like me, have chosen to lower the price of admission to their hearts even when they are not coerced or threatened. The price paid for the momentary perceived gain is completely out of balance. Some feel there is no chance of finding anything better in life, so they compromise and exchange precious items from their value system that at one time would never have been sold at all, let alone at the price they are now willing to negotiate.

The enemy of souls that I speak about in this book is the one behind it all. He is the one who calls to us. He is the one who plants fear and doubt. He is the one who fans the desire for pleasure and makes it so enticing that we may give in and respond, and pay a huge price in exchange for some sought-after item.

Addictions are rampant in society. We all have friends who are willing to pay time, money, health, and conscience for items that are worth far less than what is given in return. Addictions come in all forms, from people, pleasure, items to eat, drink, or ingest. For some, it might be in the form of items to purchase and hoard. Addictions can come in the pursuit of power or control. The desire for fame, recognition, or financial status can numb the soul and take people places they never planned to go.

As a young boy and teenager, opportunities came along for me that offered an array of intriguing things in exchange for the satisfaction of making the right decision. I'd like to be able to tell you that I never, ever made a bad purchase, but I cannot. The enemy is crafty and knows how to play the game. He puts opportunity in front of us and because the item is desired, the price is paid. There are some things we want so badly, we pay the price without much thought of the cost. We are often not able, or even willing, to look ahead and count the cost of the decisions we are making today. We want what we want, and the price is often way beyond the value of the goods.

Human nature tends to live in the moment, whereas God would like us to be more aware of the big picture and the price of admission that is required to seek after the lasting and eternal treasures we really desire.

At the beginning of my wilderness journey, as I sat in a counselor's office to sort out my thoughts and confusion, he asked me a question that I have not forgotten. He asked, "Bill, why were you willing to live life and make choices at a currency level that was well below your value system and integrity markers?" He was calling me to accountability and to the wonderful challenge and opportunity to reset my moral gauges. His question made me aware of the compromise in my own soul, and that I had been willing to lower the price I was willing to exchange for my integrity.

It's a question for all of us to remember each day as we go about life. The opportunities to test our standard of exchange are never ending. What we get to decide is whether we will lower our price of admission for personal, momentary pleasure or gain, or if we will be absolutely unwilling to negotiate on the things that really matter. For any price.

LESSONS LEARNED

1. The decision to compromise our own price of admission is personal. No one else is ever responsible for the compromise and negotiation we make with our souls.

2. The lowering of the price of admission to our souls and value systems is usually at tremendous cost to our joy, happiness, and peace. It is a very high price to pay.

3. All of us must own our decisions. No one else ever makes those choices for us.

4. We own the currency in which we deal with life, and we negotiate the price we pay for the choices we make. If we don't like the price, we should not make the exchange.

COMPASS POINTS

1. How high is the price tag on your heart and moral compass? Are you committed to that price or are you prone to compromise? Why?

2. There is always a payoff for the choices we make, or we wouldn't make them. What is the payoff you are willing to accept for exchanging life at a lower rate of moral currency?

NOTES FOR MY BACKPACK

Being at home with God is when all His resources are explored within the boundaries of integrity, honesty, commitment, trust and other values that represent Him and His desire for us. His desire and purpose for creating us was to be in relationship with Him and others. Healthy relationships happen when these boundaries are protected.

From the Wilderness

Home is the place of peace in our hearts and minds, and has nothing to do with who actually physically lives with me in the house where I eat and sleep. It is a very personal space. It is the place where God desires us to dwell, always.

From the Wilderness

We would do well to always point out to people who they really are, and who they are becoming, rather than reminding them of where they have been and how foolish it was of them to go there.

From the Wilderness

12

HOW TO LOVE A PRODIGAL

One of the most loved stories in the Bible is found in Luke 15. It is simply referred to as the story of the Prodigal Son. A prodigal is one who takes all the possessions he has and lavishly, abundantly, and recklessly squanders them. He spends money like it was never going to run out. He is wasteful and extravagant.

Jesus told the story in the book of Luke, and it goes like this. "There was a man who had two sons. And the younger of them said to his father, 'Father, give me the share of the property that is coming to me.' And he divided his property between them. Not many days later, the younger son gathered all he had and took a journey into a far country, and there he squandered his property in reckless living. And when he had spent everything, a severe famine arose in that country, and he began to be in need. So he went and hired himself to one of the citizens of that country, who sent him into his field to feed pigs. And he was longing to be fed with the pods that the pigs ate, and no one gave him anything.

"But when he came to himself, he said, 'How many of my father's hired servants have more than enough bread, but I perish here with hunger! I will arise and go to my father, and I will say to him, "Father, I have sinned against heaven and before you. I am no longer worthy to be called your son. Treat me as one of your hired servants."' And he arose and came to his father. But while he was still a long way off, his father saw him and felt compassion and he ran and embraced him and kissed him. And the son said to him, 'Father I have sinned against heaven and before you. I am no longer worthy to be called your son." But the father said to his servants, 'Bring quickly the best robe, and put it on him, and put a ring on his hand, and shoes on his feet. And bring the fattened calf and kill it, and let us eat and celebrate. For this my son was dead, and is alive again; he was lost and is found. And they began to celebrate." Luke 15:11-24

Many books, theological sermons, artist paintings and musical scores have been written based on this story. There are some personal lessons I drew from this story as I passed through my wilderness.

The far country this young man traveled to is not far from where you and I live. It is any place other than home. Home is the place of peace in our hearts and minds and has nothing to do with who physically lives with me in the house where I eat and sleep. It is a very personal space. It is the place where God desires us to dwell, always. It is here where we seek His plan and His adventure. Here, we are consciously aware of His presence and we seek His pleasure and His calling on our lives. It's a great place, one that few people leave once they have fully experienced it. And this Father's resources for providing peace and satisfaction know no limits or boundaries. Without hesitation He gives anything we would need or desire to make this home a place of vibrant peace and fulfillment.

God's resources, offered to us in abundance, include all the senses with which to take in the world around us. Eyes to see and enjoy the beauty He has created for us. Tactile nerves to feel and touch the things that He wants us to explore. Taste buds to taste the exquisite and rich flavors He has invented, and ears to hear the fabulous blend of sounds of music, birds, the familiar voice and words of a loved one, or the pure and innocent laughter of a child. All these things and more were designed to give us the feast of His description of pleasure. He gave us feelings to experience and words to share those feelings. He gave us a variety of endearing and expressive words with which to experience vulnerability and closeness to others.

Above all that, He also gave us time and energy to move about and explore the fulness of all these gifts. His resources include the ability and freedom to choose whatever experiences we might want to pursue in search of pleasure. He holds nothing back.

Being at home with God is when all His resources are explored within the boundaries of integrity, honesty, commitment, trust and other values that represent Him and His desire for us. His desire and purpose for creating us was to be in relationship with Him and others. Healthy relationships happen when these boundaries are protected.

When we are at home with Him, we desire, and fully experience His plan and His wishes, and we enjoy the pleasure of the abundant life as He meant it to be. It is a place of wondrous contentment.

Home can be experienced in a variety of ways and places. The family unit, when growing up as children with siblings, is one place. The family unit within marriage, with or without children is another. Being part of any group, church family, or part of an office or employment setting are also opportunities to enjoy His gifts within the boundaries of God's intended value systems that were designed to guard relationships. Living "at home" in this way is a beautiful place, wherever it is found.

However, often there are temptations to travel away from those safe places. There are times when we feel drawn to go to a "far country," or in other words spend His resources lavishly in ways He never intended. The human heart sometimes craves to experience those things that we believe we might be missing out on by staying at home with Him. We get enticed to believe there are exciting experiences "over there" that appeal to the senses we have been gifted with. We may ask Him if we can travel there and spend some of His resources, but more than likely, we just go there without bothering to ask, as the boy in the story did. When everything had been transferred into his account and the money was under his control, the prodigal son caught the next ride out of town. We can come to believe that because the resources are in our control they are ours to spend as we want, and we just go about using them according to our desires, hoping that maybe He won't even notice that we have slipped away from Him.

In the story of Eve and the serpent in Genesis, the serpent enticed her with the hope that she could become like God. She told the serpent that God had instructed them *not* to eat of the tree and that if they did, they would surely die. The serpent replied, "You will not surely die. For God knows that when you eat of it your eyes will be opened and you will be like God, knowing good and evil." Genesis 3:4,5. He was inviting her to leave home and visit a country far away from God's plan, and it worked. It often works with us, too.

I make no attempt to try to parallel every detail in this story to mine. However, like the prodigal son, I have not always lived a life at home with my Heavenly Father and with His plans in mind. I didn't take money to spend. I did take the God given resources meant to bring Godly pleasure and spent them outside of His boundaries, in ways that He never planned or wished for me to do. I wasted His resources on experiences that brought my human heart pleasure. Sometimes, for different reasons and at different seasons in our lives, we choose to take the tour over the border. In the story that led me to this wilderness, I was deeper into a "far country" than I had ever been in my entire life. Never before had I misused God's blessings and resources the way I had at that time. I truly wanted to find my way home to my Father and live a life of integrity again. I was not happy about where I had been, but I longed to change all that and somehow find a way to finish well.

If you are like me, you may have taken adventures into "far countries," maybe even on more than one occasion. Some regret their teenage years. Others would like to relive different chapters in their lives. It was not that they planned to abuse God's gifts, the temptations and opportunities just presented themselves and it seemed like a good idea at the time. And of course, some have openly rebelled against God and done things on purpose that they know are not part of His plan. It's the natural response of the human condition when left to follow its own desires.

Like the prodigal son, I wondered how I would be received back home. How would God receive me? How would my wife, my children, my family, my church, my friends and my co-workers receive me? I didn't know, but I had to go and find out. I had been away far too long.

In the story Jesus told, the father was beyond ecstatic that his son had come home. The son didn't even get to finish his rehearsed repentant speech before his father abruptly interrupted him and would not hear any more. He called for the servants to bring the ring, robe and sandals, all signifying a full restoration to his former position. Then he gave the orders to start getting ready for a celebration party. He kept repeating, "My son was dead and is alive again!"

What refreshing, unbelievable words those were to that son!! They were no doubt beyond his wildest imagination. He would have been happy to be a servant with just a dry place to sleep and some good food in his stomach. Instead, he got his old room in the house back, with all the privileges of being a son restored. He was a full member of the family again.

What did the father know about that son?

He knew that the son already felt shame. He knew the son had felt the full effect of failure. His health, his dignity and his integrity had been compromised. The Father's words and actions were his attempt to reverse, as far as possible, the impact of the son's actions on his own soul. But sometimes the consequences of our travels to "far countries" remain with us forever.

Having been away to a far country, I can tell you from experience that a returning prodigal does not need to be reminded of how foolish he has been. He knows, better than anyone who can remind him. I've heard it said, "A bald man does not need to be told he is bald." I can add to that and say that a prodigal does not need to be reminded of his devastating choices.

The prodigal son had hurt his father, but the father was not focused on that. Like the young man in the story, I too experienced the incredible impact of unconditional love whenever I was treated with grace as friends came to stand beside me as I trembled. They encouraged me as I began the process of healing. We would do well to always point out to people who they really are and who they are becoming rather than to keep reminding them of where they have been and how foolish it was of them to go there.

The father in the story didn't hesitate or wait for an explanation. He didn't interrogate the boy to see if he was sorry. He didn't ask if there was any money left that he might get back. He simply loved him. It is always fascinating to me that the father received his prodigal son back without hesitation or reservation. It is equally fascinating that he didn't leave him in that condition. He covered him with a robe of acceptance, a ring of authority on his finger and sandals to demonstrate his place in the family. Our Heavenly Father always receives us exactly as we are, but He never leaves us there. It is His plan to transform us into His own children who are so content to be at home they will never want to leave again. He is fully aware of what going to a "far country" costs us. He wants more for us than we are willing to even hope for.

That is the example of what God asks us to do for all returning prodigals. He explicitly shows us how to love them. He doesn't define or categorize the "country" we have traveled to. God does not categorize sin, saying THIS sin qualifies for forgiveness, but THAT sin does not. We are not to determine the depth of sin. God loves all weak, ungodly, sinful enemies.

I ask that you not confuse what I just said with the reality that there are consequences to choices made. Love and forgiveness for prodigals does not necessarily erase those consequences. Some choices end relationships permanently. Some decisions and actions put people in prison, under circumstances that we have no control over. Sometimes the returning prodigal does not enjoy the health they once had before making choices that affect it. But we can always love prodigals regardless of what else is going wrong. The resources the son wasted in the far country could never be retrieved. But despite the loss, the son was eligible to be loved by the father. What an incredible picture of God.

If we are the Father's children, do we not have a calling to love as He did?

Which brings me to the rest of the story that Jesus told. It didn't stop there with the party for the son going on. It continues.

"Now his older son was in the field, and as he came and drew near to the house, he heard music and dancing. And he called one of the servants and asked what these things meant. And he said to him, 'Your brother has come, and your father has killed the fattened calf, because he has received him back safe and sound.' But he was angry and refused to go in. His father came out and entreated him, but he answered his father, 'Look, these many years I have served you, and I never disobeyed your command, yet you never gave me a young goat, that I might celebrate with my friends. But when this son of yours came, who has devoured your property with prostitutes, you killed the fattened calf for him!' And he said to him, 'Son, you are always with me, and all that is mine is yours. It was fitting to celebrate and be glad, for this your brother was dead and is alive; he was lost and is found.'" Luke 11:25-32

The father's older son had never asked for his inheritance and had never left home. He had never wasted his father's resources. When he saw and heard of the party that was going on for the brother who had, he was furious.

We can hear him spitting out the words. "I have never left your side, and I've been home all the time. I was loyal and I was faithful. I never squandered your resources, yet you have never once celebrated or had my friends over for a party. You never killed a calf to have a feast for me, but this brother, who wasted your things, comes home and you treat him like this!"

When we look down on others who make mistakes, we are like this brother. No, he never ran away with his father's money. He may have not left physically, but he did not appreciate or live out his father's principles and values of grace and forgiveness. This father demonstrated that home with him is a place where judgment and criticism does not belong.

To go to a place of judgment or criticism of another is simply a different way to leave the Father's side and travel to the "country" of pride. "I've been good, faithful and loyal, not like this brother of mine. When do I get a reward?" The father said "Son, you are always with me, and all that is mine is yours." The reward was to always be with the most incredible father one could imagine.

Staying home with the Father is always the better life choice. Every resource is ours. Fatted calves are not needed to celebrate when we live in the presence of a loving Father all the time. Every day is appreciated. When we are at home with the Father, enjoying His presence, we do not have to navigate the consequences of guilt, broken hearts or the sad regrets that confront those who travel to "far countries."

I experienced the loving grace of the Father through those who chose to celebrate my return. I also encountered the pride of the older brother. I heard things that were being said behind my back, and I was sad, for me and for them. It's never nice to hear harsh things and judgments being made, but it was also important for me to learn to just leave that to God and let Him work with the pain in their hearts that prompted those words.

God works in wonderful ways to bring healing. One time, a man came to talk with me after he heard me speak at a men's group meeting where I shared some reflections of my journey. He said, "Bill, I'm so glad I came today and listened to you. I must confess that in the past I said things about you that were not right, I was judgmental. I am convicted today that I need to apologize to you and ask forgiveness." It was a precious moment for him and for me. It was not easy for him, but it brought freedom. I didn't know he had said those things so I was not carrying anything about it, but it was the day he stopped carrying it as he found a way to set it down and leave it there.

I have no desire to condemn or criticize "older brothers." That's not my place. Jesus counseled us against judging others, for any reason. We all must come to the Father with a humble heart. We all need to remember that being in the presence of the Father is the greatest gift of all. "Older brothers" need grace too. I'm aware that I have acted like that "older brother" far too many times in my life. Our goal should be to receive each one we meet as the father in this story did.

It is important to remember that all prodigals who come home again need loving arms, restoration of dignity, and celebration for the fact that although they have journeyed afar, they have found their way home.

LESSONS LEARNED

1. It's hard to come home when the heart is full of regret and loss. But when it's time, retracing our steps is all that matters, and nothing will get in the way.

2. There is nothing so wonderful as to be loved as the father in this story loved his son.

3. Loving as the father did can make all the difference in the world to a prodigal.

4. Judgment, like that from the older brother is devastating to a prodigal. And it is not a reflection of the Father.

COMPASS POINTS

1. Is there a prodigal you know that could use a loving word or action right now? What would keep you from acting like the loving father to that person?

2. What needs to be in place in your heart and soul to avoid rejecting people as the older brother did?

3. What relationship could you heal by expressing words of apology for the thoughts you may have carried about them in the past?

If we don't purposely choose to move forward with intention, we will often just simply fall into a life of complacency, laziness, and negativity.

From the Wilderness

Live with intention. Walk to the edge. Listen hard. Practice wellness. Play with abandon. Laugh. Choose with no regret. Appreciate your friends. Continue to learn. Do what you love. Live as if this is all there is.

Mary Anne Radmacher

When tempted to hold back and "take care," I am now instead grateful for the reminder that playing small in the world doesn't serve anyone,
especially God.

From the Wilderness

13

MR. PINSTRIPES

I first met Mr. Pinstripes sometime in the Spring or Summer of 2006. He had actually been a part of my life for many years. I just had not recognized him for who he really was.

It all started with a simple statement at lunch with a friend. He said, "My Life Coach...." and I have even forgotten what the rest of the sentence was. "Life Coach" was a new term to me, and while I didn't know exactly what that was, I was very curious.

I asked him what a Life Coach was, and he told me they are people trained to help other people find direction and ways in life to identify goals they want to achieve, and then work with and challenge them to discover strategies to accomplish those goals. They can be personal, business, or relationship goals. I was intrigued, and determined I had to find out more.

About a month later, while at lunch with a different friend, he was excited to tell me that he was taking life coach training, and that I should consider doing it. His words just came out of nowhere. This was too cool! I was fascinated by the idea a month earlier when I first heard the term, and now I knew someone who could tell me how to become a Life Coach. He told me a bit about what he was learning, where he was learning it, and how fulfilling it was. He gave me the name of the textbook he was studying and pointed me to where I should go online to order it and find out how to register for the training. That just threw gas on the smoldering idea, and the journey to become a Life Coach began.

I bought the book, and I was immediately captivated. I determined I would do whatever it took to be trained. I know I will always be a pastor in my heart. I want people to know that there is an eternity to look forward to in a much better place than we experience on planet Earth. I want them to know how to get there, and that the way is simple and already prepared. This will always be my first calling.

However, I also want people to live their best lives possible on this earth until Jesus comes and the next life begins. I am sad when I see people's God-given potential so underused and lifeless. I was excited to learn skills on how to help people in a way I had never known about before.

I registered, and two weeks later I was in Chicago, attending the first class of the training. It was challenging, insightful, extremely fascinating and rewarding. It required a commitment, and it was anything but easy. But it was worth it all as I could anticipate another doorway through which I could become involved in encouraging and assisting others.

The first part of the training was done through five separate training sessions and took approximately five months to complete. It was somewhere during those classes that I met Mr. Pinstripes. I don't recall exactly the exercise we were doing, or which class it was. We were learning about the cautious, even sometimes negative words and phrases we hear in our minds that, in effect, put brakes on all our good intentions and momentum in life. Words such as, "That will never work!", "What makes you think you will be able to accomplish that?", "Be careful now. Don't make yourself too vulnerable!" "Don't try that. If you fail, you will just make yourself look stupid!"

They even had a name for that voice. They called it *The Saboteur*. Another popular word is *The Gremlin*. The exercise had us think about where those words were coming from, and to intentionally question the source and the accuracy of them. I began to recognize my recurring negative pattern of thinking for what it truly was.

I was startled to become more aware that I had a lot of noisy chatter going on in my mind that was keeping me stuck. I was pretty much treading water without much forward momentum. Where were these thoughts and words coming from? Why did I battle them?

I don't think the exercise was designed to get to the root of that question, but rather was designed to simply help us recognize that we can be pretty hard on ourselves and fail to live with intention. If we don't determinedly choose to move forward with purpose, we will often just simply fall into a life of complacency, laziness and negativity.

It is more evidence of the human condition we are born into. Some find it easy to see the dark side of all situations that they face. People stay stuck for lots of reasons, and life can be a dreary run, as opposed to the abundant life that God would have us live.

This same exercise went on to suggest that we make use of our imagination and personify that saboteur, the source of those negative thoughts, in order to bring that "voice" to life in our minds. We were to picture someone whispering in our ear, which might help us identify the source of those thoughts a little better. I decided to have some fun with this exercise. That's when I met Mr. Pinstripes.

While I didn't ever try to picture his face in terms of details and features or describe his voice, I pictured that these negative thoughts were coming from a very well-educated man. He was logical, and very articulate, using well-thought-out language. He was professional, confident and exceptionally intelligent. I imagined him as always standing behind me, speaking over my shoulder into my ear.

I gave him the name Mr. Pinstripes after the conservative, well-fitted business suit I pictured that he would be wearing! The suit fit the tall, well-dressed and impeccably put together persona he had. It was a perfect name, and I began to chuckle. His words carried such logic. They were very convincing and hard to argue with.

I pictured Mr. Pinstripes as a man who was trying to be my friend. He had nothing in mind but his own approach to life and was full of caution at every turn. He was the one who said things like, "Don't do that, you might fail!" "Don't try that, if it doesn't work you will look silly." "Are you sure that you can take that on? Are you smart enough to accomplish all that?" "Don't get too ambitious, pace yourself well."

When I was particularly hard on myself and called myself down, it was then that I pictured Mr. Pinstripes standing behind me speaking with fluent articulation and making arguments that could not be brushed off.

Many times, especially early in my wilderness journey, I was extremely hard on myself. While I had not met Mr. Pinstripes yet, during this exercise he came to life in my mind. As the pieces started coming together, I realized that the thoughts I now pictured coming from him, were the things that kept me paralyzed. The words were very cautious and stifling and it sometimes seemed I was frozen in time.

I had thoughts such as, "Why is it that you think you have anything to offer people?" "What makes you think you can be a successful Life Coach, or that you will have anything to give to people ever again?" "What makes you think you can be a successful anything?" "You would do better to just find a job that pays the mortgage so that you can stay financially secure and keep a low profile." I realized that Mr. Pinstripes was a man of extreme caution.

It was obvious to me that thoughts and words such as these were certainly not helpful. But they were very well-spoken and even convincing if I listened and paid attention to them. They were even more convincing when I pictured that they were spoken by a well-educated, highly-skilled and polished man, Mr. Pinstripes!

Through my training as a pastor and now as a Life Coach, I know that God wants us to step out in courage and do good things for others. He wants us to have a passion for the betterment of people and the world in which we live. He wants us to do great things for Him. The Bible calls it the "Abundant Life." He wants us to experience it personally, and I knew it was becoming much clearer that my life purpose would be fulfilled in helping others achieve an "Abundant Life" as well.

Mr. Pinstripes, with his safe and stifling rhetoric, was cautious, wanting me to see that he was concerned about my safety. I pictured that in his own twisted way, he was actually presenting himself as my friend, hoping that I would understand how much he wanted to take care of me. He was simply making sure I didn't do anything more damaging with my life than I had already done. All the words I played with, as if they were from him, were meant for good. But, in reality, they were just the opposite.

As I have talked with people, I realize that everyone wrestles with these "gremlins" in their minds. That "voice" that challenges us on a continual basis to question, raise doubt, caution and check-in on everything we think and plan to do. These thoughts may just be noise in the back of our minds until we become aware of them. When we realize that these stifling thoughts can actually be addressed and challenged, we discover that we may be living a much smaller life than we are truly capable of.

Of course, there is no Mr. Pinstripes, but it was a good visual for me to remind myself that I can listen to the dark or overcautious thoughts in my mind, or I can listen to God, who wants to teach me lessons that will build and prepare me for things yet unknown in His plan for me.

I'm not suggesting Mr. Pinstripes is the devil. He is not my enemy. He is just an image that I have personified as the source of the thoughts and ideas that keep me from boldly discovering where God is leading me. No doubt the devil loves to discourage and tie up our thoughts through hesitation and fear. But picturing Mr. Pinstripes speaking over my shoulder helps me shift my attention and choose to focus on the voice of God instead. When I hear those negative things, I just smile, remembering that God is bigger than Mr. Pinstripes!

I loved discovering this. It was from this insight that I learned to be more intentional in all aspects of my life, and in service to others. I can choose to not let fear or even caution get in the way of courage and stepping out in faith. When tempted to hold back and "take care", I am now instead grateful for the reminder that playing small in the world doesn't serve anyone, especially God. It doesn't help me be of service to myself, my family, or to those who God would have me cross paths with.

I'm grateful for learning to recognize Mr. Pinstripes! We need to be very selective about who we allow to have a voice that speaks into our lives. There are many voices out there on the internet, social media, books and even friends that are not the voices from which we should take guidance.

While it was once just an exercise, now when I listen to my thoughts and give heed to the fears and logic that hold me back from doing bold things in the world, I accept that his well-intentioned arguments are only hurdles in the way of what God wants me to do and be. When I recognize the train of thought, I just smile and say, "There's Mr. Pinstripes again", and I am reminded to change my focus. Then, I look for my confident heart, and with renewed faith and courage I can truly thank God for having a purposeful use for my life. Even with my scars and wounds, I can move forward, excited to continue the adventure and not let fear master me.

I often just say out loud to my negative and cautionary thoughts, "Thank you Mr. Pinstripes for your concern and input, but God and I have got this one. We are going to move ahead in this new adventure."

LESSONS LEARNED

1. The words of caution I hear in my mind when I think of moving forward in life are only designed to hold me back from living God's Abundant Life.

2. I am determined to recognize those thoughts for what they are and let them push me to see what God in fact wants for me and from me.

3. I get to choose whether to be held back by the fears and negative thinking that I realize and recognize from time to time, or I can choose to be intentional and step through this chaos to a place of courageous action.

COMPASS POINTS

1. Where in your life are you listening to cautious, mind-numbing, fearful thoughts?

2. How is listening to these thoughts keeping you from fully experiencing an abundant life?

3. Imagine your version of Mr. Pinstripes in your life story. What do you need or want to say to him or her?

NOTES FOR MY BACKPACK

It seems to be part of the human experience that we choose to learn life's hard lessons personally, rather than be wise enough to learn them through the experience of others.

From the Wilderness

How sad if we experience painful life lessons, but ignore them and keep making them, thinking it won't be so bad next time.

From the Wilderness

14

HOW TO HIT YOUR SECOND SHOT FIRST

It happens far too often for my liking when I golf. I'll step up to take my turn for my next shot. With everything clear in my head, fully knowing what I want to do, I swing and make the shot exactly as I planned it. Well, all except for the fact that the ball does not go anywhere near where I planned on it to go. It may just bump and bounce a few short yards, or it may go right or left into trees or water. Nothing like the beautiful image I had in my mind.

Sometimes my golf buddies will say, "Take another shot," or "Take the mulligan we promised you. Don't count that one, hit again." Often when that happens, I step up again and do what I think is the very same thing, but the result is so wonderfully different. I have often seen that second shot go straighter and farther than I even dreamed on the first shot.

I have often played with an older gentleman who, in his good humor, would often say after that would happen, "Bill, you need to read the book I'm writing! It's called, 'How to Hit Your Second Shot First.'" We would laugh together and move on. As many times as he repeated that same line, it never got old. He of course was referring to the fact that if I had done the first time what I had done the second time, I would have enjoyed the benefits of it on the first shot and not needed the mulligan or the extra points on my scorecard.

Wouldn't it be great if life was that simple? Wouldn't it be great if we could do everything right the first time?

Life lessons do not come easy. It just seems to be that some of the richest, most meaningful lessons are unfortunately learned in the hardest of ways. People's lives often turn around or go in a completely new direction after some crisis moment. A close call to death can absolutely change how they drive. A spouse may give an ultimatum that "things will change, or this marriage is done," and relationships change. A doctor points to a test result or an X-ray, and people completely alter their lifestyle.

Or even worse. The result at the Doctor's office may bring the startling statement "There is nothing more we can do. You would do well to put your affairs in order." Suddenly, even immediately, the things that didn't matter before are now high priority.

During my wilderness years, I have had much time to think and meditate on life. I have spent countless hours in a vehicle traveling thousands of miles for the work I did over a period of ten years. With all that driving time, I decided to enjoy what some have called "The University of the Automobile." I spent countless hours listening to spiritual as well as daily-life-skill wisdom as I passed the miles. Many of the speakers and teachers taught me a few things about second chances and new opportunities.

In a group exercise I did one time, we were each given a "theme" song, picked just for us. Mine was "Give Me One More Shot" by the group Alabama. What a fitting song for me. The song pleaded for just one more shot, one more sunrise to give it everything I've got. All I wanted was a new shot and a new day. God, time, and life lessons have given me a second shot.

As we journey through life, we observe the lives of others. Some people teach us lessons about what we could and should do, others teach us life lessons about what we do not ever want to do. We see many things we don't want in our own lives. We see people who have made choices that have not brought them good health, or anything particularly successful or happy. It's not judgmental to pay attention to the mistakes of others and avoid those mistakes. It is judgmental to call those people losers and decide they have nothing to offer life, or ignore them altogether. We can learn life lessons in the most unexpected places.

I have known many people who have been disappointed in marriage or have hurt their marriages badly by poor choices of neglect, mental abuse, hurtful language, physical abuse, and betrayal. I have known many who have been the victims of abusive spouses or married to spouses who decided they were done with the marriage and wanted to end the relationship. No amount of talking, pleading or reasoning by a spouse or counselor was able to change that, and the marriage ended.

Seeing all that, walking beside people who experienced those things first-hand, is a reminder to pay attention to the things that matter to make a marriage strong. It never fails to amaze me that it is the tendency of the human heart to walk in a spirit of pride and carelessness that thinks, "That will never happen to me. I will be smarter than that!" That was me. I carried that attitude, and I imploded spectacularly!

I listened to a man once describe to me the horrendous, abusive mistakes of his father. Some of them had been secrets that his sisters had just uncovered. He was angry and in tears, with deep, emotional pain and disgust toward his father. You can understand the shock it was for me to find out a few years later that this very same man was found to be guilty of the exact same abusive actions toward his own children, and was suffering the same consequences.

It seems to be part of the human experience that we choose to learn life's hard lessons personally, rather than be wise enough to learn them through the experience of others. We touch areas where the sign says "wet paint." People have died testing the ice to see if it is really as dangerous as the sign says it is. I've talked to pastors about the folly of my mistakes, only to have those same people follow the same journey I took and suffer the same consequences. The examples of not learning from others are endless.

I have had many days, years, and now even decades to reflect on why and how I made decisions that led to destructive consequences. I recognize and acknowledge that whatever steps were taken, it happened in a spirit that said, "I can manage this. Others have ruined their lives, but I'll get through this." How sadly wrong I was. Journeying along, learning the lessons as I go, I cannot ignore the lesson of paying attention the first time and avoiding the consequences of arrogantly thinking "I've got this."

However, I've also learned that the hardest lessons in life are usually the most valuable ones. I've learned things in this wilderness that I could never have learned without it. I've become a person that I would never have become without the detour my life took. Do not misinterpret that to mean I am happy and proud of the journey my life took. It just means that the journey my life has taken has taught me things I may not have learned on any other path.

I do not know the life lessons learned by overcoming a life-threatening illness. I do not know the lessons learned by being charged with a criminal activity and facing a judge or jail time. But there are things to learn from each experience we face in life and each path has valuable lessons if we are willing to learn them from others.

I was in a group setting one time, where each person was talking about valuable life lessons they had learned. I will always remember the statement one lady offered. She said, "If I could go back and live my life over again, I would not change a thing. I would not want to repeat those same mistakes now, but it's those mistakes that I have lived through, and life lessons that I learned from them that have made me who I am today. I like the person I have become, and I wouldn't be here without those mistakes." I have often reflected on that comment.

There may be ideas that one might want to debate in that statement, but there is truth there as well. Each day, each victory, each failure, each painful, and each joyful experience teaches us lessons that we can use for wisdom or for ignorance in the days ahead. How sad if we experience painful life lessons, but ignore them and keep making them, thinking it won't be so bad the next time.

If we take the life lessons we learn, even in our mistakes, and use those to shift our thinking, our priorities, or our way of thinking, we have created value from the moments we would rather leave in the past. Perhaps we have become wiser. More empathetic. More forgiving of others and more compassionate toward them despite their mistakes. These are all valuable life lessons. It's just unfortunate that sometimes it takes some hard knocks to receive the value of them. My friend says, "I've graduated from the University of Hard Knocks." That sadly is the truth for too many of us. Maybe we have not all graduated, but it would be my guess that most have taken a few courses there.

Wouldn't it be great if we could always live the events of our lives without regret the first time? With no need for do-overs? If every experience, every opportunity was to just be exactly the way God meant it to be, life would be amazing. No disappointment, no pain, no need to step up and do it over again.

However, I am also glad for the God who has demonstrated Himself in the Bible, and in the lives of countless people, to be the God who gives out second chances.

Adam and Eve were offered grace. They were told they would die the day they ate the fruit, but then grace stepped in and they were given fresh opportunities. Abraham lied to preserve his own safety on more than one occasion. Jacob was the father of Israel but lived a life of family drama. David committed murder to hide his relationship with Bathsheba. Jonah ran away from God. Peter denied his relationship with Jesus by cursing and swearing. That's just a few.

Each and every time God said, "Why don't you take another shot! I'm not finished with you yet."

It's not God who has trouble with second shots. He understands the frailty of the human heart and psyche. His Son walked on this earth as a human being like you and me. He knows hunger, thirst, exhaustion, and the need for sleep. He has been tempted in every way that we have. He gets us. That does not mean that He doesn't care or that it doesn't matter if we fail or make mistakes, but it does mean that He understands.

He often spoke to people and said things like, "Your sins are forgiven, go and sin no more." But He would rather support us to get it right the first time, so that we don't have the pain and challenge that our life lessons bring us. He would love for us to "Hit our Second Shot First" every single time.

How do we do that?

Simply, pay attention and trust God when He guides us. If He says "Don't," then don't. If He says, "Do this," it's no doubt very safe and rewarding to go ahead and do it. There is always good reason to not do what He says we should not, and to go ahead and do what He says we should. In other words, take Him seriously. We are not smarter than God, as much as we would like to think we are.

We demonstrate wisdom when we learn from the lives and mistakes of others. When we see them pay with consequences for choices made, it is good to take that as a message that the same consequences will happen to us. We would do well to stay away from thinking, "I can manage it better!" We cannot. We will fail, too.

Oh, it could be argued that some have gotten away with mistakes without consequence. Specific instances could be pointed to and held up as examples. I would simply agree, and then add, "so far." The Bible says, "Be sure your sin will find you out." That says to me that we can "Be sure, your sin WILL find you out."

By the grace of God, a gracious wife, forgiving children and family, and a host of friends, I was given the chance to take a second shot at life.

In July of 2013, I was asked if I would consider pastoring a church again, on an interim basis, while a search for a permanent pastor proceeded. I readily agreed. A few weeks later, the conference president met with me and said, "I think it's time to put this whole story behind you. Let's just wait a little, while we take steps to make it more permanent." I was excited with his commitment to me and patiently waited.

Without going into detail about all the steps in between, in January of 2014, I was officially invited to pastor two churches on an interim basis, until the position would be filled permanently. I readily agreed and preached my first sermon as the interim pastor in the Seventh-day Adventist Church in Medicine Hat, Alberta that very same weekend. About three months later, I was asked to change and take up pastoral duties in the Seventh-day Adventist Church in Sylvan Lake, Alberta. Once again it was to pastor on an interim basis while they searched for a permanent replacement.

Within a matter of weeks I was called by the same president and was told, "We decided to change your interim status to permanent. You are now the official, permanent pastor of the church." I replied "Wow, I'm still trying to decide if this pastoring harness fits for me! It's been a while since I wore it!" He laughed and said, "Well, if you decide it does not fit, let us know and we will start looking again." That was the agreement, and it stayed that way until I retired just over six years later.

The Medicine Hat church, along with the Adventist church in Brooks, Alberta for just ten weeks, and the Sylvan Lake church for over six years, made me feel welcome, loved, appreciated and fully accepted. Like a prodigal, I was welcomed with open arms and was enthusiastically supported while I stepped up to take my second shot at pastoring. While the lessons continued, the wilderness felt like it was fading into the distance behind me. I was restored in many ways to what I had known before. In August of 2020, I officially retired from pastoring. This time I got to preach a farewell sermon, step away in dignity and walk with my head up and my shoulders square to the world.

God gives second chances. He gives us opportunities to hit our second shot first!

I'm paying attention to lessons learned. I have grown in ways I could never have dreamed of through the experience of it all. It has not all been easy, but it has all been rewarding. Like the lady in the group circle, I have learned things I could never have learned any other way.

If only we could take our second shot first every time and in every area of life!

Well, wait!! We can. Learn from life, learn from others. Learn from me. Learn the lessons I'm sharing in this book. Take them to heart. Forget about proving you can safely do things your own way where others before have messed up. Step up to the ball, do all the right things and hit it straight and long the first time, every time!

LESSONS LEARNED

1. Sometimes the deepest lessons are learned from the hardest of experiences. Look for the lesson instead of focusing on the pain of the classroom.

2. Remember that God always forgives anyone who wants to be forgiven. He does not want us to repeat mistakes, but He accepts humility and repentance every single time.

3. Even when He offers forgiveness, He does not always remove the consequences. However, He may also stand by and watch with a smile on His face as we hit the second shot and enjoy the fact that we got it right that time.

4. To be one of God's children, we do well to forgive readily and give people the opportunity to demonstrate lessons learned. Let them step up and take a second shot and applaud wildly when they do it well. We are not the monitor of people's behavior. We are called to love people and let God deal with the hearts.

COMPASS POINTS

1. Where in your life would you like a chance to just forget the first shot and hit again?

2. What needs to be done differently so that you get it right this time?

3. As you think back on your life, what are the learning events that have changed the trajectory of your life for the good?

4. How will life change as you search for value in the hard lessons and events of life?

NOTES FOR MY BACKPACK

What are the things you keep doing that never really fix anything, but simply keep things the way they are, or even makes them worse?

From the Wilderness

To improve is to change;
To be perfect is to change often.

Winston Churchill

Not everything that is faced can be changed,
but nothing can be changed until it is faced.

James Baldwin

15

IF NOTHING CHANGES, NOTHNG CHANGES

I used to play a game in the margins of my notebooks in college. (I wonder if that had anything to do with my mediocre G.P.A.?) When I became a little bored with the lecture that was taking place, I would doodle as I listened. Picture it with me. I would write a 1, 2, and 3 on one line, and then underneath I would write another 1, 2, and 3. Then I would attempt to draw a line from each number on the top line to each of the numbers on the bottom line without crossing any lines. So, from the 1 on the top line, it was easy to draw a line to the 1, another to the 2, and then to the 3 on the bottom line. When I went to do it from the 2, I could find a way to do that also. But no matter how I tried when I went to 3, I could not find a way to complete all the lines without having to cross over one of the previous lines. I could always get two lines from the third number, or eight in total, but could never get the last one to work.

I tried it countless times. One day after math class, I went to the teacher, drew it on the board for him and asked if it could be done. He stared at it for a few moments, then tried it and quickly concluded, "No, it can't be done on a flat plane. It could be done if you could lift one line and bend it over one of the other lines." That made sense and I could see the truth in his answer.

Guess what? Despite what the teacher said, I still tried to do it. Many times, in fact. Over and over, and nothing changed. I've never yet been able to do it, and I admit that I am aware that I never will be able to. But every now and then I still play it again, just for fun.

In my work with people, I often spend time with couples who are challenged in their relationship. One of my favorite questions to ask is, "What are the things you keep doing that never really fix anything, but simply keep things the way they are, or even makes them worse?" When they answer, I ask them how that works for them or benefits them in their lives. They quickly acknowledge that it doesn't work well at all, and there is no benefit. But like me with my math game, they keep doing it over and over, hoping there will at some time be a better result. Without judgment, I ask them as I ask of myself, "How successful is it to keep doing the same thing over and over hoping that something will change?"

I've heard a question many times in many contexts: "How is this a reflection of your life?" In other words, how is what I am doing right now, in this moment in time, a reflection of how I live my overall life? If we pause and look at some of the patterns in our lives, we may find that we play that same pattern out in many other ways as well.

If I keep trying to play a simple math game that can never be won, where else in my life am I repeating behaviors that will never have a positive outcome? And I do mean never! No matter how often I repeat it. That's a question we would all do well to ask of ourselves. There really is no good answer.

When I pause to consider the habits or ways that I live out my life, I am able to recognize patterns. If I procrastinate on taking care of business matters that are not pressing at the moment, is it possible that I procrastinate in other areas as well? With very little thought I may very well admit, "Ah, yes, I also procrastinate in taking care of clutter and putting things in their place. I procrastinate in the need to prepare ahead of time and be ready for the tasks I need to take care of. I procrastinate in making many of the changes that would really enhance my life. I recognize that procrastination shows up in several ways. And, if nothing changes, nothing changes. If I don't find ways to balance out that truth, I will be procrastinating next year or five years from now. Putting things off doesn't get me what I want in any way, but sometimes I keep pretending it's not a problem."

That's a simple example. What about the deeper games that people play with life? Where in life do we keep trying to win when there is no win available?

Relationships, especially close and intimate ones, need continual care and attention. Not only when they are broken, but also to keep them healthy. A healthy plant demonstrates nurture when it receives fertilizer, water, and sunlight, all in the right balanced amount. It takes attentive work to make it so. Imagine the gardener who knows that a certain plant needs less water than another plant in the garden but chooses to just give every plant the same amount. The gardener might think, "It's just easier to spray water on them all at the same time and it will all be ok!" After a time that plant is not flourishing while the others are. Why? Because the gardener could not be bothered to pay attention to what that plant required.

It is a very sad fact that many relationships die, simply because at least one or both parties do not care enough to find out, and then do what nurtures the growth of the relationship. Sometimes they do know, but for some inexplicable reason, they simply choose not to put the energy into taking care of the needs of the relationship that are right there in front of them, begging for attention.

One of the things I cannot help but notice is the determination of people to prove that they are "Right!" Demanding that the other person give in because "I know what I'm talking about" never wins. I have played the "I'm Right" perspective in too many situations and it's as futile as my number challenge. There is no way to win that game.

Being determined to be "Right" in any argument has the potential for conflict. Being determined to be right in EVERY argument has potential for never-ending conflict, irreparable damage, or divorce. It's amazing to me what happens when hearts soften and say, "Sure, I appreciate your perspective, that looks like a good idea. Let's do it your way."

Gwen and I laugh a lot about how different we are when it comes to going about doing things. The way we drive from home to a given location in town is never the same. The way we wash the car, the way we vacuum the floor, the way we do almost anything. But neither of us is right, or wrong. Just different.

I heard a statement once that says: "Everyone is right, but only partially." It's a good reminder to do everything we can to work to get along with others. The peace that exists is much more rewarding than the tension or silence when one never feels that their input or ideas are valuable.

One year, when I was on the road a lot, I met a few too many police officers, if you know what I mean! Eventually I received a personal letter from the Alberta Government respectfully admonishing me for the four speeding tickets I had received in the last ten months and that if I did not alter my driving habits I was in danger of losing my license for a time. (Sort of like, "If you collect four of these the prize is a bicycle!")

I realized that I needed to change things, and I also needed a bit of a margin, because I was to the point that if I got stopped at any time during the next year for something as simple as not fully stopping at a stop sign, I would not be able to continue to drive. I decided to attend a six-hour safe driving course by which, upon completion, I was able to go straight to the registries office and buy back some points that would create the margin I needed. I took their letter to heart and since then I have adjusted my driving habits back to a clean record again. (Just in case you were wondering!)

I am telling you this because at that course the instructor emphasized the goal of all drivers is to simply be committed to share the available space on the highway. He mentioned it several times throughout the day. Simple. "Share the space." Trucks, cars, motorcycles, motor homes, all have a right to be on the highway at the same time. What we don't have the right to do is demand to take over the space that someone else needs at the very moment they need it. I've experienced or watched road rage incidents. I've watched drivers not move over for others who are merging. I know from experience what it is like to attempt to merge and have people not allow me in. There would be so much more peace on the highways, and in the world if we could all learn to share the space and leave the need to be right out of our habit patterns. In driving, as well as all aspects of life. Road rage has ended in fatalities. Life rage has also ended in fatalities. How sad, all because someone could not allow another to be right in that given moment.

To my amazement, I watch couples disintegrate into anger right before my eyes as they spend all their energy on winning and getting the other person to see how right they are. The effort is to get the person to see it from their perspective, with the belief that if "you see it from where I see it, you will understand why I am right. You will then give in, and we will be happy." Do you see any challenge to the relationship here? When the other person is not willing or able to see it that way, then anger takes over. And we all know that when anger sets in, words are said that would not otherwise be said. Angry emotion is not a good framework for constructive discussion and progress of any kind.

Another tactic that never seems to win is silence. When a relationship is in a conflict and there does not seem to be a way through, often one or both partners will decide that silence would teach the other a lesson and they stop talking. It is obvious that sometimes a "time out" in a conversation might be valuable if emotions are causing grief or getting out of control. However, many people go silent in order to win, and determine with dug-in heels that they will not be the next one to talk. It's a different version of "I'm Right." I have heard it said that sometimes "Silence is violence." When one is determined to be right and win, the outcome is never rewarding. Think about it. If you win, the other person loses, and no one likes to lose. So, you have won the thing you were fighting for, but the relationship has taken a hit. The one who loses is bruised and tender and possibly moves into a space of cordial distance. Talking is still happening but the distance is hurtful.

I was traveling one time and staying in a hotel. In the evening, I called Gwen to catch up at the end of the day, as was my habit. For whatever reason, she was not in a chatty mood and the conversation was not gaining any momentum. Finally, I simply said, "Well, when you feel like talking, why don't you call me back." And I hung up. I was sure that I had certainly put her in her place, and that no doubt she would be calling right back to apologize. I believed I was right, and surely with a little thought she would admit that I was right. My silence would definitely make my point.

I waited for the phone to ring. It didn't. I waited for at least a half hour. Finally, I picked up the phone and called her to apologize. My quick, abrupt words and my silence were a desperate attempt to manipulate her into feeling foolish to the point she would for sure call. That is another pattern you might find if you look inside with honest accountability. How often do you use words for the purpose of control and manipulation of the situation? And if it shows up here, where else does it show up? Does it also happen with friends, or at work? How we do anything is often how we do everything.

When I called and apologized, we had a much better conversation. I had wanted to be right, and prove I was right, and that always ends poorly. However, it required me to check my ego and decide whether I wanted to keep doing what I was doing and remain distant, or I could set my pride aside, acknowledge my poor attitude and create an atmosphere for growth and closeness. It was up to me. I could choose to "be right," or I could choose to do the right thing.

It's always up to us. So many relationships are damaged because one or both are unwilling to lay down their swords and find a way to talk, listen and learn. Like nurturing a plant with the right amount of ingredients needed, it takes continued effort to be a close parent, friend, or spouse. It takes diligent work, and it is a work that never ends, but it's the best work one can engage in. The rewards are beyond what one can imagine.

One of the simplest and most beautiful skills I have learned is to say to people, "The thing I like best about you today is......" and finish the sentence. It's incredible how much that simple phrase can do. Saying it to children makes them crave more. It makes them want to do things that bring about a compliment like that. We have gone around the table before or at the end of a special meal and each one said to the person beside us, "The thing I like best about you today is...." What a great way to experience a sweet time together.

I know of a wife who decided to do that with her husband. For two nights she told him what she liked about him that day, and he would listen and then simply shrug his shoulders and say, "Okay." On the third night she shut all the lights off without saying anything and he said, "I think you forgot something. You didn't tell me what you liked about me today." She said, "you're right," turned the lights back on and proceeded. This time he responded and said, "And the thing I like best about you is......" The conversation opened up and the heart sharing went deep. That is when the intimacy of the soul can really blossom.

How would things change if people really listened to each other more? One of Stephen Covey's habits for highly successful people is, "Seek First to Understand, Then to Be Understood." What a gift that could be when the tension begins to escalate. If one would say, "I'm going to be quiet and just listen to what you are wanting to get across to me. Please tell me what it is you want me to hear." When that person is done, it would then be appropriate to share their thoughts in response. And, how great it would be if the person who spoke first wanted to really hear what the other was saying and where they were coming from.

When it's very clear what each is asking for or expressing, it's so much easier to then find a solution that wins for everyone. When win-win takes place, neither party is off in the corner nursing their hurt while the other is proud of their "success."

It takes ongoing, intentional work. It takes humility. It may require an apology or the willingness to let others choose sometimes. It takes gentleness and sometimes holding the tongue. Not every thought that enters our heads needs to come out of our mouths. Life could be much sweeter if we regularly check on our verbal and emotional filters to make sure they are in place, and in good working condition.

It may require slowing a conversation down, especially when emotions are high. If the goal remains to build a relationship, it is crucial that both parties in the relationship receive the care that is required. It is what keeps both parties engaged and committed. When one person feels cut off, shut down, unable to ever have any respected input, the desire to work and try to build healthy intimacy is choked off completely.

I am saddened at some of the things I observe as people try to make headway. I think of a couple where the mother was crying out for gentleness and tenderness for the children, and the dad was determined that discipline was the way that children learned respect. He was just as sure that her lack of discipline was as dangerous as she was sure that his harsh, exacting leadership would do damage. We talked for several meetings with very little or no change on either perspective. It could be so much better to seek to find a mutual parenting page, one they could both be committed to. But when nothing changes, nothing changes.

And it goes deeper than parenting and relationships. It's also very personal. No matter how close we are to a spouse or partner or a child or a parent, we are the only one we are with twenty-four hours of every day. We know what we do and have done each minute of each day, and no one is privy to that information unless we tell them. And even when we tell them, we are unable to duplicate every thought, motive and nuance of each event. It's just not possible.

Sometimes it's a bit of a loop, too. We get into personal patterns that don't get us what we really want or need from life and then we can be very hard on ourselves. We remind ourselves continually of the things we do wrong and the losers that we really are. We play back events and experiences that we are not proud of. Maybe we refer to things we said in the heat of the moment and now in the quietness of our minds we admit that it was neither kind nor necessary. But the pattern is to beat on ourselves, maybe many times for the same thing. It provides no value and only works to steal our own joy and confidence.

I think of a time when I drove out of a lane in a shopping mall parking lot. I saw a vehicle coming from my left and I was turning right. I had time to turn but as I turned, I realized the vehicle was coming much faster than I first realized. I was now in front and suddenly the driver was right up behind me. The driver blasted me with her horn to let me know how much she disapproved of my driving skills. Since we were now in a lane that she had to follow me for a while, I decided that if she wanted to honk at me, I would give her something to honk at, and I slowed right down. I received the result I expected. She continued to honk, and I continued to go slow. As soon as she got to a place that she could turn off, she did so. And, just as soon as she turned and left, I reflected for a moment and asked myself, "Now, why was that necessary?" It wasn't necessary! An "I'm Right" attitude had risen up in me in a flash as I excused myself because I truly didn't mean to cut her off when I pulled out in the first place.

Nobody was there to experience that event, but I was still disappointed in what I had just done and didn't feel good about my actions. In the end, the situation brought me no joy or satisfaction and if I knew who she was, I would apologize to her now. However, if I don't change that, next time a similar opportunity arises, and I repeat the action, I will feel the same regret all over again. If nothing changes, nothing changes.

It's one thing to notice what needs to change, it's another thing to change it. If both people in a relationship are willing to stop doing the things that don't work in the relationship, everything could be different, instantly! If apologies were offered, it could change many things. If people would prove themselves trustworthy, trust could be rebuilt. It's not complicated, but it is discipline and ongoing relationship work. It's the nurturing of the plant in balanced ways. The relationship looks healthy because it is healthy. The relationship stays healthy because the people in the relationship are busy working it. Pride is set down. Ego is ignored. Forgiveness is offered and accepted. It's a beautiful thing, and because changes are made, everything changes.

All that I have shared is theory that I have made every attempt to put into practice as I have worked to rebuild my marriage relationship. I can tell you from personal experience that it works. I have worked hard at making every necessary change in order to give Gwen security and reason to trust me. While the thoughts I have shared are skills I have learned from reading, study and experience from helping others, I can also attest to the personal satisfaction of seeing it displayed in my own personal life. Making change where change is needed is absolutely necessary to experience the results I am searching for.

I leave you with a challenge. What things do you know in your heart that you need to do differently? This is not about what the other person needs to change. It's about taking responsibility for your side of the street and making sure it's in good shape. That's the work. The rewards are amazing. What changes are you willing to make?

LESSONS LEARNED

1. Recognizing the statement that "If nothing changes, nothing changes" is a great reminder to be willing to adjust.

2. Being willing to adjust, lay my sword down and work in constructive ways with the people in my life can shift relationships from tension to fulfillment.

3. Learning to stop repeating things that are never successful gives us an opportunity to start looking for the things that will get us more of what we are searching for in relationships and life in general.

COMPASS POINTS

1. What are the things that you know in your heart that you need to do differently?

2. How willing are you to take responsibility for your role in all aspects of your life?

3. What changes are you willing to make?

4. When will you start making them?

NOTES FOR MY BACKPACK

Norman didn't need a main part to make a difference.
He just made a difference through the role
he created for himself.

From the Wilderness

The world is round; what seems like the end
could be just the beginning.

Unknown

16

NORMAN

I read the story of Norman in a book called *Messy Spirituality*, by Michael Yaconelli. I'm retelling the story now as I remember reading it. I am not able to verify any part of this story or where it even took place. I don't know if the little boy's real name was Norman or not, but it was Norman in the telling of the story as I read it.

Norman was a schoolboy in a class where the teacher announced that they would be doing a school play and that it would be the story of *Cinderella*. Excited hands went up everywhere as the children called out for the parts they wanted to play in the story. Decisions were made. Finally the teacher came to the last boy and said, "Norman, all the main parts are taken, but I'm sure we can find a part for you. What part would you like to have?"

Norman said, "I want to be the pig!"

The teacher said, "Well, there is no pig in the story of Cinderella."

"There is now!" said Norman.

The wise teacher didn't know what that meant but she said, "OK, you can be the pig."

Norman created a pig costume and made up his own role, which was to follow Cinderella all over the stage and physically mirror the emotions that she might be feeling at the time. If Cinderella was sad, Norman the pig would drop his head and slump down sadly as he wandered around after her on the stage. When Cinderella was happy or excited, Norman would respond accordingly and would wiggle with excitement as he made his presence known. At the end of the story, when Cinderella and the handsome prince left together, Norman the pig was so excited that he stood up on his hind legs and barked like a dog as he danced around!

Because there was no script, he could do whatever he wanted. The teacher took him aside and said, "Norman, I really like what you are doing. It's very good. But, Norman, pigs don't bark!"

Norman responded, "Well, this one does!"

The teacher conceded and said, "OK, you can bark like a dog."

The big night came. The audience was there, and Norman did his part with enthusiasm. At the end of the story, Norman danced around and barked like a dog, just as he planned.

After the play, at the curtain call, it was not Cinderella, or the handsome prince, but Norman who got a standing ovation!! The crowd loved him and his creativity.

That story caught my attention and made me smile from somewhere deep within my soul. I too, loved his creativity and the spunkiness within him that created a pig in a story where there was no pig, and a pig that barked when pigs don't bark.

I connected with the story so deeply that I shared it with my Life Coach. She listened, and like a good coach, explored with me what it was that made this story stand out. Then she asked the question that made it come alive for me. (Of course, that's what she is supposed to do! It's what a good coach does!)

She asked, "So Bill, where is the Norman in you? What is the part in the world's story that you still need to create?"

That was such a great challenge for me! In the wilderness where I was now existing, nothing was familiar, and everything was so far from the career I had trained for and the world I had oriented my life around. The thought that a new script could be written, designed specifically for me, was a wonderful, adventurous thought that lit up my imagination. What did God yet want from me? What could God yet do with my life? What could yet be designed that I could do that would allow me to serve people for the kingdom of God? Maybe even in a way that no one had done or even thought of before!

The answer to that question is still unfolding and continues to offer clarity, but the question still burns in and guides my thoughts. In my mind, I often hear my coach's voice as she asks me, "Where's the Norman in you, Bill?"

When I think of that, I turn the question to God and ask, "What do You want from me now? Where can I serve You now? What do You yet want to create through me for the people of your kingdom?"

That keeps me looking forward. It helps me stay focused as my new story continues to be written.

In the early days of my wilderness, long before I met Norman, or my Life Coach, I was taking life one step and one day at a time. I had no other training than that of a pastor and I needed an income to take care of simple things like a mortgage and food on the table. I was paying attention to my heart and the healing of my life and relationships, and I was also looking for meaningful employment.

The day on the golf course, when the lawyer planted the seed for mediation training, was a gift that opened doors that I had never thought of before. I had no idea such a career existed and had to ask him what mediation was. I drove home, and immediately went to the internet. I searched and found the course I was looking for. I looked at the requirements, the cost, and the time it would take and found it all very doable. I didn't know about Norman then, but I was, like him, creating my own path forward. I wasn't just going to settle for a job to simply pay my bills, I was going to construct one. It was my way of creating a new role in the world for myself.

I was soon registered and in September of 2000 I began a series of classes that prepared me for the work of mediation. I successfully completed the requirements and passed the two exams by February 2001. Through contacts I made while in training, I was offered a temporary position that has opened doors which have given me opportunities I would have never dreamed of while simply searching the employment ads in the newspapers. Because of this training, I have been invited to work with schools and churches that have struggled with conflict and division.

Gwen and I had attended the *Choices* seminar in November of 2000 and found it incredibly helpful in the growth and healing of our relationship. Two years later, in November of 2002 I was hired by *Choices* to do marketing and support for their workshop, a work I loved and was blessed to do for the next 10 years. I was in that training room countless times through those years, learning each time how people can be blessed when they are loved and accepted and given an opportunity to make choices that would help them receive more of what they wanted in life. By "more" I mean finding freedom from pain left over from their childhood or past life. Finding the ability to address regrets and failures. Experiencing deeper satisfaction in their present relationships. Discovering ways to really connect and nurture relationships with their children. More joy, more fun, more "aliveness" every day. Simply, more of the things that really matter in life.

In 2007, I was certified as a Life Coach and have met many wonderful people as I have walked beside them through their life experiences. Here, I found another place to encourage people and seek to challenge their growth in life with questions such as my coach had asked me. All I wanted was to be someone who could create ways to bless others.

Do you see the trend? Each of those platforms for work involved working with and encouraging people to live successful and fulfilled lives. The very thing that God would want for each one of us on the planet. The nature of my work in any of those venues allowed them to dovetail nicely together and I grew to love the ways I was able to serve, even though it was from a different place than I had been used to or originally studied and prepared for. I was not able to work formally as a pastor, but my pastor's heart was always alive and present, searching for ways to influence people's lives in positive ways.

I realized, as I journeyed, that God had not left me to flounder and "figure it all out on my own!" He had in fact provided opportunities for me to learn things that I wished I had known many years earlier. I wished that every pastor I knew could learn the listening skills and processing skills that mediation training had taught me. I wished that everyone I knew could learn the life skills the *Choices* seminar taught as I and thousands of others had experienced healing and growth there. Like Norman, I had discovered a whole new part in the story of life where I could be of service to others. It was marvelous.

Even though I never read the Norman story until years into the wilderness, the Norman in me found that there is more than one way to make an impact in the world. Norman didn't need a main part to make a difference, and neither did I. He just made a difference through the role he created for himself. I realized I could do the same thing. I was in a place I had never planned on, but I was in a place that was fulfilling to my soul as I enjoyed every day.

I am still watching for ways to bring exciting challenges into my interactions with people. I still have the Kingdom of God firmly in my mind and vision as I journey through life. I thank God that He provided places for me to still befriend, love and care for people and to fulfill my life's calling. While very different from where I started, even in the wilderness His calling and leadership was still very obvious. Like an oasis, His opportunities have provided much enjoyment, even in the dry places I was journeying through.

LESSONS LEARNED

1. When it seems that there is no evident part that is available to play, It does not mean that there is no part to play!

2. If my part in the "play" is not clear, I can accept the challenge to explore resources that God would have me use to create a new and yet unwritten part of my life that would bring glory to Him and His kingdom.

3. God does not sideline people, but He does restore them. I learned that I should always think outside the box to find the purpose that He would yet have me fulfill.

COMPASS POINTS

1. What hinders you from discovering new and rewarding roles for you to engage in?

2. How will you go about discovering the Norman in you?

3. What is your part in the world's story that you yet need to create and fill?

It’s not the options we have before us that get us into trouble, it's the decisions and choices we make with those options that can really bring grief.

From the Wilderness

Every decision you make–every decision–is not a decision about what to do. It’s a decision about Who You Are. When you see this, when you understand it, everything changes. You begin to see life in a new way. All events, occurrences, and situations turn into opportunities to do what you came here to do.

Neale Donald Walsch

17

THERE IS ALWAYS A CHOICE

I have a friend who often says, "I have given up all hope of having a better past." When did you last do something that really made no sense now that you look back on it? The question keeping me awake many nights was, "What were you thinking?"

As I stumbled along in my wilderness, I looked under every rock to find a really good excuse or reason for why I was there at all. In all my searching, I could not find one. I was lost and confused. A few months earlier, I had been enjoying work that was part of my heart and soul. My work was a calling on my life, and it was right and real for me. But now I was totally disoriented.

It was easy to make up stories and assumptions about what people thought of me. Why wouldn't they think harsh and negative thoughts? I desperately wanted people to know that in many ways, I really was a pretty good guy. I wanted to talk to everyone I knew, all at the same time. I desperately needed them to understand that what they heard about me, or now knew about me, or thought they knew about me, was really not the real me. It was all defensive, of course.

One night, very early into this journey, I was laying in my bed, wide awake in the middle of the night. I was desperate to talk to someone, anyone! Who could I think of that would answer their phone at 3 a.m.? I remembered reading in a book that any man could probably easily identify six people to carry his casket, but how many men could name one person they could call at three a.m.? I was trying to think of one!

I picked a friend who had been empathetic to my heart in this situation and had promised that I could call anytime if I needed to. I called the number. There was no answer. I left a message and sadly hung up. Now what? Within a couple of minutes my phone rang. It was him. I had awakened him with my phone call and he was getting himself oriented before he called back. It was so great to hear his voice.

I babbled on about the stuff that was on my mind and shared my emotions and tears with him. He was a good listener. I was ashamed of myself and not afraid to say so, but I also wanted him to know that underneath it all I still was a pretty good guy. I so wanted to believe in myself and I needed someone else to believe in me as well. I wanted him to know that there were extenuating circumstances involved, things he didn't know about, and I wanted to explain. I just could not come to the place of openly admitting I had really messed up and had totally blown my own life apart. I was avoiding accountability.

When I stopped rambling and gave him a chance to talk, he shared from his life experience for a while. Then he said something that I have never forgotten. I don't remember the context of his statement, but I remember he said to me that in his life journey he had adopted a mantra that said, "Don't explain and don't complain."

I paused to let those words sink in. I recognized there was truth there, but I needed time to process it. I didn't know if I was complaining, but I was certainly doing a lot of explaining. "Don't explain and don't complain." He repeated the words.

I could feel myself relaxing, settling somehow. It wasn't because I was happy, but because I was surrendering. I was surrendering to the truth and the acceptance of the truth. There was no excuse, no one or no circumstance to blame for my poor choices. I could not pass this off. I was a free moral agent who had made choices which had sabotaged and self-destroyed my own integrity and freedom.

As hard as that was to accept, surrender to that truth brought a relaxing sigh. To admit that and say it out loud produced a sweet freedom.

He continued as he expanded his thoughts and went on to say that complaining about how others might view me, or see me, or think about me was not honoring them. In fact, it was actually judging them, when I was the one responsible for what had happened. Explaining to them was only rationalizing and was not honoring to myself or to God. Whichever side I focused on, I was sidestepping the real issue. In the middle of the night, on that phone call, I realized that it was time to take ownership of my own self-implosion. I had to admit that regardless of temptation, opportunity or circumstance, I always had choices, and I had made poor ones.

We hung up the phone and I went back to bed. I thought about that conversation until I drifted back to sleep. Since that call, I have often remembered his words and I still hear his voice saying, "Don't explain and don't complain!"

St. Augustine prayed, "O Lord, deliver me from the lust of always vindicating myself."

Explaining and complaining play out in many ways on a regular basis. When I have been late for an appointment, I want to explain why. When I haven't called someone that I said I would, I want to explain. When I have not followed through on a commitment I have made, I want to explain. I want the person to know that it was circumstances beyond my control that kept me from accomplishing what I said I would do. It is true that sometimes circumstances do make following through impossible, but often we use circumstances to excuse the truth that we simply did not plan well enough in order to keep the commitment.

Coupled with that is the strong desire to be right. Who wants to be wrong? If we have done something we should not have, or have not done something we should have done that we need to apologize for, we are forced to admit that we are guilty! The human heart recoils at the thought of admission of guilt! We would rather attempt to come up with all types of explanations about why we are not responsible under the circumstances.

I had another opportunity to practice this skill. I sometimes heard things people were saying about me. It wasn't easy. I was tempted to defend (explain) or react (complain) in some way. There were some hard days.

I remember speaking to my pastor about a hurtful event that had just happened, and I have not forgotten his wise advice. He said, "Just absorb it, Bill. Don't retaliate. Just let it die within you." Then he went on to remind me that when Jesus died on Calvary, He took all our sin onto Himself, and absorbed it. It died there with Him with no revenge, response or retaliation. And He was innocent, where I was not.

I got the message. If Jesus did not complain, why should I?

Learning to absorb unpleasant things and let it all die with me was just another way of stopping the search to blame or defend. Simply letting it all die was another way of surrendering, and it did feel really satisfying.

We have choices on how well we keep our word and whether or not people can count on us. We often make flippant promises. "Sure, I'll do that." "Let's get together." "I'll call you." "Mark me down for that." Often, we don't follow through and instead shrug our empty words off. If we aren't careful, our casual nature and lack of follow through can eventually make it so that people don't trust our word and feel they can't count on us anymore. It's up to us and it is our choice.

And there are the bigger promises in life, as well. Like when we promise, "I do," on our wedding day. Or when we have children. By bringing them into the world, we make inferred promises to them that we will love and protect them until they are able to take care of themselves. When we sign up for employment, we are also promising our employers to put in honest work for the pay we receive from them. But too often we make the choice to not follow through and we search for reasons to hang our excuses on.

We continually face a barrage of choices in every area of our lives. The question is, what will we do with those choices? It's not the options we have before us that get us into trouble, it's the decisions and choices we make with those options that can really bring grief. Every single time! We either end up content or we end up with regrets!

The sad reality is that sometimes those choices are made in full awareness of the possible consequences of those decisions. The human mind works amazingly fast and we can rationalize at lightning speed. Rationalization looks for ways to ignore those consequences and allows us to make poor choices anyway. We are so good at excuses we can even find ways to make poor decisions knowing ahead of time the excuses we will use if it does not turn out well. We can be very creative when we feel the need to explain. We want people to understand that of course there was "my childhood, my parents, my siblings, my circumstances, my history, my friends, my teachers, my colleagues," and the list becomes never-ending. By choosing to justify, we simply sidestep the reality that we own the choices we make. One of the choices that is always available is to just do the right thing. That was the lesson I learned the night my friend taught me, "Don't complain, and don't explain."

And when we don't do the right thing even when it is hard, it's difficult to just admit, "My life is where it is because I made the choices that got me here." That is a place of integrity!

Instead of excuses, we are better people if we can simply say:

"I'm not healthy because I don't eat good food and I don't exercise."

"My house is cluttered because I don't work to clean it up and keep it clean."

"I'm overweight because I don't do what I need to do to lose the weight I need to lose."

"My relationship is dysfunctional because I participate in the dysfunction of it, and I don't do what it takes to create the boundaries necessary to live in a healthy and happy atmosphere."

My choices took me into my wilderness. After that 3 A.M. call, a new peace began to settle in. Just own it. It truly was time to give up all hope of having a better past and focus on what it would take to finish well.

It was a lesson that we can apply in other ways as well.

If we find ourselves in poor relationships that aren't working, what will we do to change it? Instead of waiting for the other person to make the change, why not choose to focus on what we are doing that needs changing?

If we are stuck in jobs where we don't like the boss, the co-worker, the job itself or the working conditions, what are we accountable for that we need to change? It may be as simple as making the choice to adjust our attitude, or doing the hard work of finding a more rewarding job. It is always up to us.

If we find ourselves in a standoff with a child or a teen-ager, we don't have to be pushovers, but we may be contributing to the issues by insisting on being right all the time. What choice could we make that would make a difference in the way we parent our children?

If we are distant and far from God in terms of a meaningful relationship with Him, what needs to change, and where do we need to start? What choices are available?

We are accountable for our whole life! No one else can be, and no one else should be!

Back to the statement, "I've given up all hope of having a better past!" Peace starts when we accept the past that was. No amount of complaining and no amount of explaining will change the reality and the truth of that past. It's locked in. The good news is that while there may be some chapters in our lives that we cannot re-write, one chapter, or even several chapters in our lives do not tell the whole story. No single chapter defines a whole life. We may not be able to change what is already written, but we get to determine how the story ends.

Owning the unflattering chapters is where and when we begin to heal. Now the steps forward can focus on two things. What choices did I make that brought me here, and what do I need to do differently to get me to where I want to go? There is always a choice.

LESSONS LEARNED

1. When faced with my own truth, explaining why I made poor choices was only making excuses for those poor choices.

2. When faced with my own truth, complaining about the circumstances I found myself in was only an exercise in blame, and an attempt to sidestep the truth.

3. Whenever we face options or temptations, we always have a choice. The options are many, but one option is always to simply do the right thing.

4. Honesty and acknowledgement is the doorway to freedom. That is when we step into the place of power with which to deal with the truth.

COMPASS POINTS

1. Where in your life are you avoiding accountability for something by complaining or explaining?

2. In what area of your life do you need to change something so that the situation can shift or heal? What keeps you from doing that?

3. What would change if you stopped trying to create a better past and instead focused on finishing well?

The writing of a new story or a new perspective does not erase what has already been done. However, what is in the past does not have to define the rest of our life story either.

From the Wilderness

At any given moment you have the power to say,
'This is not how the story is going to end.'

Unknown

When we deny the story, it defines us.
When we own the story, we can write
a brave new ending.

Brené Brown

18

WRITE A NEW STORY

In the early days of my wilderness journey, all I could think about was all of my losses, my future and my embarrassment. I had also convinced myself that everyone else was thinking about it as well. That's how unhealthy shame works. Not only did it consume me; I was convinced that it no doubt consumed everyone else, too!

This led to some strange behavior. Since I assumed that everyone else was thinking, condemning, and talking about me, I went on to assume that they needed or wanted to know what I was thinking. I had reduced my entire life down to one unflattering chapter, and referred to that chapter as if it was my whole life. My story. Whenever I would talk seriously to anyone, I would somehow bring it around to "my story" of disappointment and failure. After all, I was sure that's what they were thinking about anyway as they spoke to me. I was stuck there.

In November of 2000, about seven months into my wilderness journey, some very good friends made it possible for my wife and I to attend *Choices,* a life-skills workshop in Calgary. It was an amazing experience and we both learned some relationship tools and skills that really helped to process this place in life in which we found ourselves. During those five days, as I worked through the different experiential learning events, I filtered everything I did through my shame, my loss and my story of failure. Some of the learning work that week was done in smaller groups of five or six, and two coaches to assist us. I no doubt wore my group out as no matter what topic we started on, I could always find a way to bring it around to "my story!" and talk from that place once again. I was consumed with it. I was in tears many times and it was all from a desperate sadness that had taken a deep hold in my heart.

It was during the summer of 2005 that I was introduced to the world of Life Coaching. One friend mentioned the word, which I knew nothing about. I discovered that another friend was studying it and had all the answers about how to register and get started in the program. About two months later, in October, I was in Chicago for my first of five training events that would teach me the foundational life coaching skills. I finished the other four in Calgary.

In April of 2006, after I completed the basic training, I enrolled in the follow up certification portion of the course that would give me the designation of a Certified Professional Co-Active Coach. It was a six-month course where I was part of a class of nine students spread from British Columbia to Stockholm, Sweden. There were students from Alberta, Ontario, South Carolina, England, and Norway as well. We met by telephone once a week and it was a profound experience to learn with people from other countries.

One of the requirements of the training was that I needed to hire a personal life coach of my own. The purpose of having my own coach was to have someone to give me feedback and direction during the program, and also to experience having a personal life coach of my own. She had taken the same course before me and was there to mentor me through the certification process.

In my first session with my coach I said, "I'm going to give you an overview of my whole life so that as we work together you will be able to relate to the full picture of who I am." With that, I gave a brief description of my childhood and foundational values. I spoke of my wife and family, as well as my pastoral career and where all that had taken me. And, because I was so fixated on it, I then included my story of failure. It was still a story on which too much of my attention was focused. I continued to be stuck in that chapter of my life. I had a very full life, a great family, a wonderful wife, fabulous daughters, and yet that dark chapter of my life was what I referred to whenever I used the phrase, "my story."

It is a sad fact that we tend to more often remember the negative things that are said to us rather than the positive. People can share a lot of good things with us about what we are or do, but if they say anything that we interpret as negative, that is what we tend to hear and remember. This was exactly what I was doing to myself. I was consumed with that one failure and was defining my whole life by it.

As well as being required to have a personal Life Coach as part of my training, I was also required to complete a certain number of hours of coaching. My mentor coach was to hear about my experiences with my coaching clients and critique my progress. With the client's full permission, I would chat over my coaching sessions with her to get feedback for learning and guidance on how to improve my skills. It was going well, and I was enjoying it all very much.

As I was coaching one of my clients, I used "my story" as a learning point for the discussion we were having. I forget now how it even came up, and it was not a major talking point, but I believed it was appropriate to talk about it for the learning moment we were in. The next time I spoke with my coach about my work, I told her about my latest coaching appointment, and I said, "I shared 'my story' with my client." I went on to tell her about the conversation.

My coach knew exactly what I meant, and that I was referring to the story of my failure. She stopped me in my tracks with a question that became a moment that I will never forget! She challenged me by asking, "When are you going to stop referring to that part of your life as "your story"? That was 6 years ago, and you have done so much learning and healing and have come so far in those six years. You have so many things going for you. When are you going to start telling your new story, and start referring to "your story" as a reference to your whole life, including what you are accomplishing now?"

It was like she slapped me; the effect was so emphatic! She was SO right! I often say, "she cut me off at my knees" with that question. I was fixated on what had gone wrong in my life instead of what was going well now. I began to wonder why I was willing to stay stuck in the chapter of my life that I was least proud of when so many things were so much brighter? When was I going to start telling my "new" story?

I can still hear her voice in my mind whenever I repeat that question to myself. It always reminds me to think about the future and what is going well, as opposed to the darkness and brokenness of the past.

And, I wonder how God must feel when we stay focused on our past instead of walking with Him into the bigger plans He has for us. I want to listen to His perspective of me, remind myself of who He says I am, and what He believes is possible, instead of staying stuck in the unflattering past.

I am fully aware that the writing of a new story or a new perspective does not erase what has been done. However, what is in the past does not have to define the rest of our life story either. We have all read biographies or fictional novels of heroes and heroines. Inevitably, there comes a chapter that takes a dark and twisted turn. The main character may commit an act or do something that is very troubling or mysterious. That is not the time we throw the book down and say, "I don't want to read this anymore!" Instead, that is the time that we become even more curious to find out what happens next and we can't wait to find out how the story ends.

What is even more exciting, is that in our own story we get to write the ending by the new choices we continue to make. I get to direct the ending of my story and write it the way I want to. I get to finish well, if I choose to.

If every year or experience in our lives was written up as a chapter in our biography, those chapters already lived cannot be re-written. I cannot rip out any one chapter because I'm embarrassed about it. However, to define the rest of my life by referring to the dark chapter as "my story" is equivalent to writing a note at the end of each chapter of my biography that says, "My life is working really well at this point, but be sure to reread chapter X, the story of darkness in my life, so that you know who I REALLY am!" How foolish would that be? The darkest chapters in everyone's life finally come to an end and then comes the new next chapter. When the book is finished and closed, then we can say, "And that's my story." All of it together, not just a chapter here or there. A hard and disappointing chapter here, or a brilliant and successful one there does not capture the essence of it. It must be taken in full.

Ever since my coach asked me that question, I have made a point to refer to "my story" as all the pieces, including that which is going well in my life. New training opportunities that are unfolding and the lessons being built into my character are as much of it as any other part. My story includes training events I have utilized to create opportunities in my life and the work I have done to enhance the restoration of relationships. It includes forgiveness and the attitudes that have shifted in my mind toward myself and my past decisions. My story also embraces the joy I have found in my relationship with God as I have accepted His grace and forgiveness for me. And I cannot minimize the realization that even some of those embarrassing parts of my life have made an impact on people as a part of the full story. As they have watched me write a new story, they tell me that they have been inspired to write a new story in their lives as well.

Who I have become, and continue to become, is all influenced by the lessons I have learned through my wilderness time. I am who I am today because of the lessons I have learned in all the chapters in my life. There are many things I appreciate about what I have learned. Who I am today includes all the chapters of the overall story.

Gwen and I were on vacation one summer. We had a day of driving, and we were having a good discussion about life in general and our lives in particular. I asked her a question to ponder: "Which would you prefer; to go back to life before I had to leave ministry, or to have life the way we have it now, including the chapter that brought us to where we are?"

She was quiet for a long time as she thought about it, and then finally said, "This may sound crazy, but I like where we are now. We have learned so much. We have learned how to talk differently. We have learned how to listen. We are closer and stronger than ever before. I don't know if we would have this any other way than going through the hard days." Oh, if only there was a way to get the learning without having to attend all the classrooms that get us that degree!

Sometimes, hearing the stories of others provides insight that people highly value. In 2002, I was volunteering at the *Choices* seminar that my wife and I had attended two years earlier. I was having lunch with the owner, and she suggested that because of that chapter in my life, I would have an understanding and compassion for people that I could never have gained any other way. She said this was the type of person she wanted around the seminar. The next day, I was offered an opportunity that began a deep friendship and a ten-year employment relationship with *Choices*. She was inclusive in her thinking, and instead of distancing herself from me because of that story of failure in my life, she embraced who I was becoming. She saw me for the story I was writing, not for my past. That was incredibly refreshing and affirming for someone who at one time could only see his life story as one defined by failure!

The beautiful opportunity for each of us is that we all have the chance to live beyond "our story", regardless of what it might be. This truth can become real in many ways. People with a simple, poor, or maybe even abusive childhood can rise and become powerful leaders as they attempt to right the wrong done to them. Many people who have been abused or bullied have become advocates for those who continue to be treated poorly.

Others, who have had no opportunity for education, have found creative ways to make it happen and have demonstrated a resilience that has taken them places that surpass those who have had even more resources available. There are outstanding biographical stories of people who have shown what is possible when they made the choice to live beyond their poverty or abandonment, sickness, addiction, or abuse, and achieve what was in front of them, rather than stay connected to what was behind them.

I am always interested in people. I want them to know that there is ALWAYS more ahead to look forward to. It means unhooking from the past story and stepping into the new story. I hope you who read this make that decision, regardless of the chapters in your past. The new story can begin right now! It matters not where one has been, we can always find our way home and finish well.

LESSONS LEARNED

1. A story of failure does not define a whole life. As dark as it might be, to define the whole story by one chapter in that story is narrow, focused, and harsh.

2. When failure happens and cannot be re-written, it can be built upon. The Bible refers to it as "beauty from ashes". We each get to choose if we want to reference our lives around our past or around the new story that we are writing.

3. I cannot control what others think of me, but it is my choice whether to stay stuck in the old story or write a new story. I am the only one who can control where I put my thoughts, emotional energy, and focus.

COMPASS POINTS

1. What dark and regretful moments in your past still define your focus, thinking and your story?

2. What things are going well in your life and what accomplishments have you enjoyed since the event(s) that carry your dark regrets?

3. Which events do you focus on or leave out when you tell your true story? Why is this?

4. What becomes lost when you define your life by the dark chapters only? What changes when you include all the chapters of your complete story?

5. How does your complete story impact or inspire others?

6. What do you want the ending of your story to look like?

Do or do not. There is no try.

Yoda

Let what you say be simply 'Yes' or 'No.'

Jesus--Matthew 7:37

I'm not telling you it's going to be easy
I'm telling you it's going to be worth it.

Unknown

19

THERE IS NO TRY

I know that procrastination is a problem for some, including me. I bought a book on the topic years ago, and never did read it! I meant to but couldn't find the time! I can't even find the book now. It seems to be a part of human nature to put things off. Some have a hard time stepping into the habit of taking care of matters at hand, while others seem to find it easy and second nature.

It's true that some tasks are of the nature that it doesn't really matter if they ever get done. Do I really need to make a stepped path to the bottom of the hill behind my house? I'd like to, but if I don't ever do it, nothing in my life will change overall.

Then there are things that should be addressed, but whether it's done today, this week, next month or even next year won't really change things either. The garage or the storage room needs sorting, but right now the sun is out, and it is summer and there are much more fun things to give my time to. I'll get to it when I can. The garden shed could use a coat of paint. Someday I'll do that.

These decisions may not need to be high on the priority list.

Ah, but then there are those things that need attention, and they cannot be put off. The question is, do we recognize which ones? Will we give them the attention they need and at the right time?

As a pastor, a mediator and a life coach, I have had the opportunity to dialog with people who are experiencing low or challenging times. Maybe their health is not good. Their relationships aren't working as they once were. The jobs they go to every day are far from energizing.

The question is always, "Is this something that you put off paying attention to, or is this something that needs to be addressed sooner rather than later?" One of the best examples of this dilemma is something that we can ALL relate to at some point or other. It's the "snooze" button. Who doesn't want to linger under the warm blankets for just five more minutes, and then five more, and maybe even five more after that?

Why are we reluctant to do the right thing when we need to? I certainly lived for a time, failing to do what was the right thing. I know what I am talking about. What is our hesitancy?

No doubt there is a payoff for waiting. Why would we continue in any habit or lifestyle pattern unless there was a payoff of some kind to it? We do not need to be reminded that we should change bad health habits. Maybe we should be exercising more. We might do well if we stopped eating or drinking certain things. We know better, but we do it anyway! Why?

It's always because of the payoff. We enjoy the taste. We don't have the discipline or the energy, which means we would rather keep doing what we are doing. We enjoy the stimulation. There is always a reason, whether we acknowledge what that reason is or not. It's that reason that keeps us from stepping up to do what we know we need to do.

I am not a science fiction fan. I have not watched Star Wars, and probably never will. It's just not in my category of interest. However, I have heard of the Star Wars character named Yoda who has a famous quote. "Do or do not. There is no try."

Procrastination is evident when we make a half-hearted effort at things. We appease our souls by promising ourselves that we will "try to do that tomorrow, or next week." All those words do is extend the decision that must ultimately be made.

What is "try"? "I'll try to call you sometime next week." "Let's try to make a plan." "I'll try to commit to that date." Yoda nailed it. "Do or do not. There is no try."

How much time is wasted just by allowing "try" into our vocabulary. There really is no such thing as "try". We either do, or we do not. If I am "trying," I am already doing it. When I say, "I will try to hit this golf ball over the pond," I follow that up by putting the ball on the ground, then swinging a club and hitting it. The "trying" part here is the attempt to hit it straight enough and far enough to clear the pond. The "try" here is for accuracy, but the action is in fact happening. To say, "I will try to golf next week" is a different kind of "try".

If I say, "I will try to make the right decision when the time comes," I'm just playing with my own mind. "I will try to take my wife on a weekly date," is an exercise that opens the door to let myself off the hook if I don't follow through.

I have learned on my journey that life is much more successful if we stop "trying" and start committing to the things we plan to do. "I will take care of my health, starting today, and these are the steps I will take." "I will make plans to meet up with you next week. Let's set a time right now." Even Jesus counseled, "Let what you say be simply 'Yes" or "No." Matthew 5:37.

And just as important, is learning to say no to the things we know we won't commit to or won't follow through on in the end. "I will not be able to make the commitment you are asking of me. I will have to say no, thank you," is a much more respectable and polite response than brushing it off with, "I'll try to make that happen," when we know we probably won't.

How often do we procrastinate on the really important decisions in life that can have a huge, maybe even eternal impact?

One of the greatest excuses for putting things off is that "I just don't have time." "When I get more time, I'll play with my children, and give them the attention they deserve." "When I get more time, I'll pay more attention to my relationship with my spouse." "When I get more time, I'll get serious about my relationship with God." "I'll pray more, when I have more time."

I bought a one-hour hourglass. It's a great reminder of how time works. There are many lessons in an hourglass. As I watch the sand run into the bottom, I am reminded that the sand piling up there is history. It represents all the decisions I've made and all the places I've been. It is a record of words spoken and actions taken. It represents the things I'm proud of and the things I wish were different.

However, the sand in the bottom never goes back up to the top for a do-over. It's history! Forever!

The sand in the top of the hourglass represents the life yet to be lived. It represents the future. When I look closely, I realize that it is falling through that tiny opening at a regulated but never-ending, steady pace. It can't be stopped, or even slowed down. There is only so much time left to do the things that need to be done. And it's running out. I don't mean to be dramatic, but I'm just reminding us all of the fact that the seconds and minutes and hours know no rush, and neither do they know slow moments. They steadily pass without procrastinating even one moment. We need to stop "trying" to do the things we want to do and get busy doing them.

Billy Jacobs is quoted to say, "Time is an illusion. It is man's attempt to measure memories and expectations. The only real, true moment is now. Embrace it for it is already a memory."

That is so true. The sand going through the middle of the hourglass is the momentary opportunity to do the things that need to be done. Those moments come, and just like that, they are gone. While we make excuses and plans to try to get them done when we have more time, moments come and go. And they are truly gone. They went from future to history in a moment.

As the sand falls through the hourglass, time is not multiplied. Sand does not miraculously and steadily multiply and replace itself in the top half. There is a certain amount of sand, and when it is gone, that is all there is.

Bucket lists are great, but I am referring to more than a checklist of fun things to do. To have things to do and places to go before we die is wonderful. I hope that you get to jump out of an airplane or go bungee jumping if that is what's on your list. Maybe it's to stand on all the world's continents. Maybe it is to walk across Canada, or even the equivalent mileage of that journey. I hope you get to accomplish every one of the items on that list.

I also hope that on that bucket list are the things that are the most important in all of life. Who needs to hear a word of forgiveness from you? Who needs to hear an apology from you? What spouse needs to have your listening ear, and a softer response when you talk? What child needs a few minutes of uninterrupted time on a regular basis, no matter how busy you are? What employer needs a more honest day's work from you? What needs to be made right or corrected?

"Do or Do Not. There is no try."

In October of 2007, I began attending a four-retreat, extensive leadership course, that I have referred to in other chapters. One of the challenges was to climb a tree to a thirty-foot platform with the harness strapped in such a way that the connecting rope was on my back, where I couldn't see it. When arriving at the platform, the task at hand was to walk the diving board that was there and leap off into thin air, trusting the rope to hold me secure.

I made up my mind that this was not something I needed to do. But at my classmates' urging, I decided that to get the most out of the course I should push myself through my fears and do what was expected and planned for me.

I climbed the tree and stood on the platform. With terror written all over my face, I began walking the plank to jump off into thin air, praying the rope would hold. The rope held. I am here to tell you about it. It was an incredibly invigorating experience. I was in awe of the sense of accomplishment for days. It can still motivate me even this many years later.

Recently, I found a journal entry I wrote within minutes of getting my feet back on the ground. My words resonate totally with the lessons I am pointing out in this chapter. I journaled: "When I decided I could and would do it, I focused forward and not backward, or on anything else. The challenge was to 'get up that ladder and do this.' I have learned that to focus on the task at hand is a gift that teaches us how powerful we can be."

As I journey along on my path, these lessons stand out to me. I have remembered how I often settled for "trying" when it was just an excuse to make myself feel better. It was like I was at least making some sort of effort to do the right thing when in reality it was only a half effort to avoid falling into the trap of total procrastination. I should have changed course at different times and places in life. I should have made decisive choices. I did not.

I have learned from Yoda. I have learned there is no "try". I agree with what I learned in the *Choices* program, "Trying is Lying." How much better it is, that when God and life call to us, we just do it! Whatever it is, but the things that really matter especially. These are the actions and the priority items that must not be put off for another time. These are the goals that must be accomplished in order to make a difference in our lives for the health and wellbeing of our families. The details that will make a difference to God, and His kingdom. Let's stop "trying" and say "yes" or "no." Do or do not!

LESSONS LEARNED

1. Pretending I'll do it at a more convenient time is not commitment.

2. Making the hard decisions, and doing them, are the things successful people do. Taking the time to pay attention to relationship details in all areas of life, and doing them, brings a satisfaction that cannot be found by always taking the easy, shallow way.

3. Life works much better when the word "try" is taken out of the vocabulary.

4. Saying "Yes" and doing it and saying "No" when I know I should not or cannot commit brings a lot of peace. Avoiding a decisive decision by saying "I'll try" is not satisfying to anyone. Even to God.

COMPASS POINTS

1. What might you be putting off for when you have more time?

2. How would life be better if you stopped promising you will "try" to take care of that, and just did it?

3. What area of your life needs attention right now? What keeps you from stepping up and doing what it takes to make a difference, right now?

THERE IS NO TRY

NOTES FOR MY BACKPACK

Get busy living or get busy dying.

Andy Dufresne

Where has your life been small and safe, compared to fulfilled, passionate and alive for the good of others?

From the Wilderness

We do well to live our lives to the satisfaction of only two people. The eight-year-old within us who finds nothing short of excitement and passion in everything. And the eighty-year-old within us who wants nothing more than to look back with peace at the way life was lived.

Unknown

Whatever your hand finds to do,
do it with your might.

Ecclesiastes 9:10

20

GET BUSY LIVING

A few recent years ago, life was bleak and dark for a while, but for a whole different reason than my wilderness story. I was afraid and anxious about everything, and it all had to do with my fear of dying. I was focused on dying and was constantly fixated that my death was going to be soon, too young, and with many dreams left unfulfilled.

I have had a few health challenges at different times throughout my life, and at that time it seemed to me that they were going to just overwhelm me, and I would die sooner rather than later. The way I felt some days made me feel pretty sure that I could not go on like that for many more years, let alone decades. It was a hard time.

I was having a visit with the owner of the *Choices* program, who has had a great impact on my life story through the years. I was sharing with her some of my thoughts and fears. She laughingly said, "Get over yourself Bill, get used to it. You are going to die! The question is, will you really live before you die?" It was one of those questions that gave me much to think about.

Close to the same time, I was browsing in a bookstore and noticed a book entitled, *2 Do Before I Die* by Michael Ogden and Chris Day. In the context of that recent conversation, the title of this book caught my eye. I bought the book and realized that no matter how many days I had left, I could spend them worrying about dying, or I could spend them focused on living. Really living! Neither choice would probably add to the number of days in my life, but my quality of life would be very different depending on which path I chose.

I am fully aware that studies have shown that stress and anxiety do have a physiological impact on the quality of life we experience, for sure. So, the choice to spend my days fully alive seemed a much better approach. The heaviness seemed to lift, and I began to move forward in a much better frame of mind.

I have watched the movie *The Shawshank Redemption*. It is about a man who was charged, convicted and sent to prison for murdering his wife. It was a mistake, and he was unfairly serving time for a crime that he had not committed. The lead character, Andy Dufresne, spent many years in jail making a strong, positive impression on fellow inmates. Due to his banking background the warden hired him to do the prison's and his own personal accounting, and in the process Andy discovered that the warden was embezzling money.

What the warden did not know, was that Andy came up with a way to steal money from the money the warden was stealing, and he quietly went about his work. While doing this, he also developed a plan for his escape and his future. Not long before he put it all into action, Andy said to his best friend, "It comes down to a simple choice. Get busy living or get busy dying." The next day he put his plan into action and in the beauty of movies and script writing, Andy's escape was flawless, and he ended his days on a beach in Mexico, well financed, fixing boats and living out his dream.

That line has a truth in it. From this very moment, until we breathe our last breath, we have a choice. We get to choose how to fill each of those days. We can choose to fill our lives with choices that are geared to simply please the body, taste buds, and the mind, only to discover that, in reality, they have no lasting value. We can fill our days with anxiety and worry. We can fill our days with heaviness and darkness. We can do things that bring temporary happiness, only to discover that it was for a shallow and momentary measure of success. But we also have other options.

We can choose to fill our days in ways which take on a realization that is bigger than we can imagine. We can make decisions that feed our bodies in healthy ways, not just our taste buds. We can choose to live in ways that measure success in things that make a positive difference to the world around us, instead of simply feeding our personal pleasure or bank accounts. We can live to make an impact in the life of a child, a friend or a group. We can live a life with passion and energy for the benefit of others and do what it takes to leave a legacy behind. There is an old Cherokee proverb that says, "When you were born, you cried, and the world rejoiced. Live your life so that when you die, the world cries and you rejoice." That provides a great reminder and lens for looking at how we might live each day of our lives.

I have a bucket list of things I would like to do. It includes some of the normal, expected things. There are places I would like to see and cultures I would like to experience. I have always wanted to see Switzerland and Israel. I have taken an interest in World War II history, and I would like to see some sites in Europe such as the beaches of Normandy, Vimy Ridge, and Flanders Field. As strange as it might seem for some, I would like to personally visit Auschwitz. I have friends who have walked the Camino de Santiago across Spain and I would love to do that or accomplish something like that.

I have much room to learn some skills in the kitchen that have not been given much priority. I can make a pretty good bowl of popcorn, an edible porridge, a great peanut butter and jam sandwich, and I can brew tea. I am capable of using the blender to make a breakfast smoothie and I have figured out how to heat up a frozen pizza, but that is a pretty limited diet. There are some things I could be interested in learning in that department.

I have an extensive library and many books I still want to read. I have much to learn, and I want to be learning when I die. As one person said, I want to "slide into my grave sideways." I agree with that, and I choose to be living a full life until it's over.

In the Fall of 2007, during the Leadership course, we did an exercise that was extremely challenging, and yet, at the same time very enlightening to me. There were twelve of us in a group and we were to imagine ourselves on a boat that was sinking with only one lifeboat available. Only three could fit in the boat. We were told there would be no exceptions, like hanging off the sides or piling people in. Only three. We were each given one minute to make an appeal as to why we should be one of the three chosen to secure a seat in the lifeboat. We could say whatever we wanted. It was an incredibly challenging assignment to have one minute to convince others to give up their spot in the boat and let me live.

After everyone had given their speech, the group was to vote, one by one, to determine who would make it into the boat and who would not. To increase the impact, we were to tell each other why we voted for them, or why we did not vote for them. It was a very transparent exercise, the kind of thing we do not do on an everyday basis. I loved the forthright honesty of it all.

In the end, I was not voted by the group to be one of the three who were saved. I do not recall what I said to the group, but I wrote down their feedback in my journal. Some of the reasons given for not voting me into the lifeboat were: "No compelling heart vision." "No heart or passion." "I could not feel what you were saying." "Your words missed passion and content."

That was a wakeup call to me and after I had written down their feedback in my journal, I also wrote a question to myself: "So, where has my heart gone?"

As we debriefed that whole process in the follow-up group discussion the next day, I told them about not being voted into the lifeboat and what I had written in my journal. The leader challenged me with one of those "juicy" questions when he queried: "So, Bill, where HAS your heart gone?"

This group knew nothing about me or my background. We were going to be together four times, five days each time, but this was the second day of the first retreat. We were all strangers still, trying to get everyone's names figured out. They waited as I processed what I was about to say. After a few silent moments I finally spilled my heart and said, "I was a pastor who made a serious mistake, fatal to my calling and career. I became involved in a relationship outside of my marriage, and I guess I've been so afraid of ever making another mistake I've shut my heart right off. I've crushed it. As I think about it, as a result of that exercise last night, and your question now, I realize that I have put layers of protection around my heart, my feelings and my passion for life to make sure I would never do anything I would regret, ever again. In the process, I can now see that I've also stopped being free to let any passion or feelings of any kind be given a place for expression."

It was more than a light bulb moment; it was like lasers going off in my brain. It was suddenly very clear how small my life had become and why no one had sensed any heart vision from me. No heart passion, no feelings or content. Just dead words. I realized I had a decision to make. I could get busy living again, or I could keep on living with a dead heart!

Since then, and through some of the learning events and experiences I am sharing in this book, I am on a continual search for the ways to live life wide open and on purpose. I want my heart to be alive and my life to make a difference in the world, not just make a whimper and then be gone. It's not good enough to just live for me and my pleasure and then be finished.

I ask the same question of you. Where has your life been small and safe, compared to fulfilled, passionate and alive for the good of others? Where is your heart? Is it wrapped up and strangled in the fear of making a mistake? Do you have life, freedom, joy and passion that has room for expression?

You may have heard of Red Green. He is a Canadian comedian who was the lead character in the *Red Green Show*. His handyman tricks and creative inventions are always novel and mostly useless, but his effort at efficiency is quite noteworthy. His style of humor is an acquired taste and to those who like it, he is quite entertaining in his own quirky way. He has often made me laugh out loud. For example, his view and philosophy of life is very simple. "All you need in life is duct tape and WD40. If it moves and it shouldn't, use the duct tape. If it doesn't move and it should, use the WD40!" Simple!

One time he was on a tour to promote his new book, "*How to Do Everything, by the Man Who Should Know*." I decided I should go, get the book, and personally meet the man. I stood in line and when I got to him, I asked him a question as he was autographing my book. "So, Red, from a man with such a vast storehouse of knowledge such as yours, from your life experience, what is your number one piece of advice?" I was playing with him, knowing that humor was his game. I was suggesting that all his quirky ways and inventions would provide a humorous twist of insight for the rest of us.

He surprised me at how fast he responded. Without a moment's hesitation he fired back at me, "Lighten up, Bill." That was all he said, but I got the message. His bottom-line piece of advice was essentially saying, "Don't take life so seriously." So many of us make life unnecessarily heavy. We can quickly see the deficits in life instead of the assets. We can quickly find and judge what's wrong with another person, event, or product, rather than find what's good or positive. And we can tell ourselves that our version of life and events are "the truth" of the matter, and never be open to changing that version.

How much better for us personally, and for all around us, if we would just lighten up a little.

Do not hear me say that we should view life as a joke, and that we should go through it frivolously. I am suggesting that if we did not take ourselves, and life so seriously, we could bring more energy to the world. Look for the fun, laugh more, and enjoy as many moments as is absolutely possible. We never know how many moments we actually have. How many have said, "If I had known that was the last day with _____________, I would have said or done things differently." What if we could just do what it takes to live without regrets regardless of what tomorrow brings?

We are not the one designated to fix the world's problems. We have not been asked to be responsible for, or the policemen of other people's good or bad choices. We are not in charge of the world, or to see that true justice is carried out in all things. God is still the One in charge, and we are not Him. Our greatest task is to let Him manage the world around us and not spend so much time thinking it through and figuring out how it should be done. So many are weary from taking on responsibilities that were never theirs to be in charge of. It's a heavy load. If we could just "lighten up" a bit, our lively spirits would surface again, and we would be much more contagious to others.

God, my family, my friends and the world around me are looking for my heart, more than my fears and heaviness. When Jesus was asked, "Teacher, which is the great commandment in the law?", Jesus answered this way. "You shall love the LORD your God with all your heart, with all your soul and with all your mind. . .. And the second answer is like it: "You shall love your neighbor as yourself." Matthew 22:36-39. NKJV.

He calls to the mind, but he calls to the heart and soul, too. He calls to our emotions and our passions. He calls out to all of us. He wants the heart and the mind connected and involved. Every part of us. And He does not want us stuck on ourselves. He wants us to simply love our neighbors (everyone else) and make it our intent to love them as much as we love ourselves.

This is really living. Jesus said He wants us to live a full life. He said it this way. "I came that they may have life and have it abundantly." John 10:10

I may not know the full extent of what an abundant life looks like, but I'm sure it's not one where we are stuck in our fears and our problems. It's not one where our hearts are wrapped tight, several layers thick like a swaddled baby. There is no joy if every day we are afraid that we cannot be excited about the lives we are enjoying. It is a life lived with purpose, full of quality, meaning and adventure. A life of passion, lived with a lot of heart involved as well.

One of the four big questions of life is, "What is my purpose for being here? Is there a reason for being alive?" Depending on our world view, the answer to this will vary. I spoke to a man once who believed there was no purpose, that there would simply come a day when planet earth would just drift off out of orbit, spin toward the sun and we would all just burn up. In a moment, it would all be over. There was no reason why we were here, and it was just a matter of time until we would all be no more. It was rather depressing to him as he spoke it, and it was also depressing to me as I listened.

I am convinced that we are here on purpose, at the hand of a designer. He doesn't make junk, and He doesn't put life within and watch to see if we can figure out what to do with it. While things are not completely the way He planned it, a Creator has brought us into existence and has a purpose for each one of us. There are many powerful ways in which we can explore and give of ourselves to the adventure of a life filled with meaning.

That requires a bucket list of a different kind. Besides all the fun and adventure we might want to have before we are done, what are the things we want to accomplish that will make the world cry when we leave? How much thought is given to our legacy?

What if, before we die, we planted a tree for a purpose, in a strategic place that made it stand out and was a reminder of something good, long after we are not there to water and nurture it? What if we left a mark on someone's life in some creative way that they were simply unable to forget it? That's what really living is all about. I have learned the value of living the fullest life possible. My challenge to myself, and to you, is to lighten up, get busy living and fill every day with something that matters. Really matters. Bring joy to yourself as you bring joy to others. Be friendly to people you don't know.

It could be really simple, and it doesn't have to involve money. Do something to make a child's day extra special, so that they exclaim, "Best Day Ever!" Listen to the story of, and encourage, one who is in their senior years. Learn from the wisdom of a lonely, elderly soul. It will not be forgotten by anyone who got to tell their life story to someone that gave them a listening ear. Call up friends you haven't talked to in ages. Volunteer somewhere. Take a community class both to meet new people and to learn a new skill. Be a missionary. Do something scary, that pushes you out of your comfort zone a bit. Read a book that teaches something worthwhile, not just the latest novel, as fun as those might be. When life happens like that, God will smile, too.

He wants our bucket lists to include Him in some capacity, loving His creation in all its forms. People, animals, nature and our planet. He wants us to enjoy living in such a way that we can leave an imprint for good when we are gone, and so that the world cries when we leave because there will be a piece missing. And when we get to that time, we can look back and say, "It was a rich and full life. I'm glad I got to live it."

Let's all get busy living!

LESSONS LEARNED

1. Unless the heart and the words are connected, there is little passion.

2. Lighten up. We are not in charge of the world. We would do well to stop living as if we are.

3. The days are going by at the same speed regardless of what age we are. We don't know how many days have been allotted to us. We cannot get back what is gone, but we can get busy really living, for the rest of the days we do have.

4. The things I enjoy doing are not the only things that matter. If I can do things for others too, life really comes alive.

COMPASS POINTS

1. What would be your one-minute speech to earn a place on the lifeboat? How would the passion and aliveness in you be conveyed that would make it a "slam-dunk" decision?

2. What makes you come alive and enjoy your days?

3. What are the "people things" on your bucket list that bring passion to your soul?

Tell your story with your whole heart.

Brené Brown

Ever read someone's story and think,
'That is exactly what I needed to hear today?'
Your story will do that for someone else.

Unknown

Nobody can tell my story the way I tell my story.
The question is, which version of me do I allow
to tell that story?

From the Wilderness

21

WHICH ME TELLS MY STORY?

One of the decisions I must make every morning when I wake up is what my attitude will be for the event or day that I am facing. I realize that some people really struggle with finding positivity in their thoughts and attitude towards life. Life can be a struggle to just find something to be happy about.

One definition of attitude is "an inward feeling expressed by behavior." John Maxwell *"The Winning Attitude"* page 20. Attitude is such a powerful gift and tool in our lives. In Viktor Frankl's book, "*Man's Search for Meaning,*" he speaks about his time in the Auschwitz extermination camp during World War II. He said that he decided they could take his dignity and even his life, but they could not take his attitude. He was determined to never let them take that one thing away from him, as it was the last thing he could control. He did survive and his story gives us a glimpse into the power of the human mind when faced with incredible challenges.

I have been blessed with a positive heart towards life. When dark times come, I am usually able to see the opportunities first. I'm the classic "glass half full" kind of guy. It's not that I never have a bad day, and I can struggle with the dark side of situations on occasion, but it's not the typical response of my mind or my heart.

In the early, chaotic days of my wilderness journey, I was completely confused, and many emotions were fighting for mastery of my thoughts. I was sad and I was full of shame. I was broken and I felt very alone in a big world. I experienced anger and the need to explain. I wanted to find resolution and I wanted answers to the questions of what would happen to me next. However, at the same time, I was always very hopeful and positive as well. I was determined to not live out my days in this dark, miserable wilderness.

Despite all the confusion, I found that my attitude kept me focused on one thing: You will find a way through this! This is not going to destroy you. There is a life to rebuild and there is a future to experience, whatever it may look like. I decided I could stay stuck in my chaos, or I could create a future. That approach helped me discover that there was a blank page in front of me, and while I didn't exactly know where to begin, it was ready for me to create something artistic. It was clear that I wanted it to be something powerful, progressive, and rewarding.

I have a mantra that keeps coming up in different places and circumstances. I often say, "I get to choose my attitude, so, I may as well choose a good one." A good attitude can change everything. If it's cloudy or rainy and I had my heart set on something outdoors, I can choose a good attitude and find something else to do with the gift of time. If things don't happen as fast as I would like, I can choose the attitude that searches for lessons and gifts from the experience. Attitude is ours to choose on any given day.

Nobody can tell my story the way I tell my story. The question is, which version of me do I allow to tell that story? I have discovered that there are many versions of me that want to find a voice and speak from some specific place in my heart and mind. Those different versions of me speak with a variety of attitude options. When I choose to pair up a strong attitude with a confident version of me who wants to speak, it can be a very powerful thing. Let me explain.

The courageous version of me, for example, was able to see my future from a place of a positive, never-give up attitude. This version of me wanted to build on the interests and skills I had already learned up to that point in my life, and actively continue to search in order to find and create more. The courageous me could only see the finish line and be determined to cross it with my head held high. I experienced an attitude of determination and grit that would not let anything stop me. I was sure that I could get on with filling in the gaps with amazing things and there was no holding back.

But if I didn't make a conscious choice, sometimes, the victim version of me wanted to just rise up, blame others and complain. That was the version of me with a dark attitude that searched for all the things wrong with life, people, and organizations. If allowed, the dark, accusing attitude could easily find the steering wheel in my mind and take me to damaging places where I knew that I did not want to go, but somehow felt powerless to resist for a time. It was not a place I chose to be, but in those moments I needed to acknowledge that I had allowed that "victim" version of me to control my thoughts and my life. That was when I would remember and rehearse things people said about me, and grumble about actions taken by some that were hurtful, and I would dwell on those for a time. A negative attitude, left unchecked for a time, can do much damage before a healthier one gets to have control again.

The frightened me showed up from time to time. I found myself questioning whether I would ever find a future that was meaningful and uplifting. I pictured myself driving a delivery truck to convenience stores, delivering potato chips and chocolate bars, because it was something that I would be able to learn easily enough. The fearful me continued to whisper that I would lose all my friends and that I would spend the rest of my life as an outcast. It was a totally fear-based attitude that took me often to a place of anguish and locked me into a reclusive mindset.

Sometimes the angry me would arise and fill my mind with a bitter attitude. I could get down on myself, and many times I would look in the mirror and spit out the question, "How could you have been so stupid?" I was hard on myself and beat myself up over my willingness to ignore my own value system's warning signs, and the unwillingness to see ahead to the ultimate consequences of my decisions. The angry me would never lead anywhere positive. That dark attitude in my heart towards myself had no place to go except to spiral downward. Anger is a bitter pill, and it only hurts our own hearts when we allow it to fester and grow. But it shows up if we let it sometimes and, when allowed, it always does its sinister work.

There are other versions of me that like to speak as well sometimes, and each of these voices represents my attitude. I like it when the thankful me speaks. Even when things are not going well, there is always something to be thankful for, should I choose to search for it. The Bible says to "count it all joy when you meet trials of various kinds, for you know that the testing of your faith produces steadfastness." James 1:2. There are gifts that can be identified in every situation, and when we focus on the gifts from the moment, instead of the problem of the moment, it is incredibly powerful to witness what can be accomplished. Having a positive attitude changes everything.

Through my experience and lessons learned, by the grace of God I have been able to sustain an attitude that has helped me through the moments of darkness. In the early days of the wilderness, it was easy to seek an outlet to blame for my circumstances, but that dropped off when I was able to look directly into the mirror and face myself.

One time I was invited to travel to the United States to give a presentation at a pastor's meeting. I was asked to share my journey for the purpose of being transparent about how as pastor's we could relate to real life temptation and experience. I was to talk to the pastors about the danger of compromising our values and integrity. It was a very personal presentation, not easy to make.

A leader, who held a significant position in my church, was present at that meeting. I had never met him personally before, but I knew who he was. He took me aside before I spoke and cautioned me. "I have been told and I understand why you have been invited to this meeting. I hope you are not going to spend your time bashing the church." I was surprised at his concern and assured him that I had nothing to "bash" the church about, nor was I going to do that. I assured him that I was well aware that it was not that I had been wronged, but that I was the one who had been wrong. I had hurt the church; the church had not hurt me. I am not sure, but he maybe experienced someone in the past who had lashed out at the church in some way, instead of accepting accountability. It was another opportunity for attitude to do its work.

I spoke openly to that group and was candid about my failure and poor choices as a pastor. Gwen sat in the front row in front of me and her presence created an authenticity to my presentation. After the meeting was over, he came to me again, thanked me, and told me he thought I should do that same thing at every opportunity I received. He told me that if I ever did this again that I should always have Gwen with me as her presence gave it all a measure of credibility. I guess he was able to relate to the vulnerable and honest version of me that I allowed to speak that day. He was confident that I was not interested in letting the angry or bitter me say what I wanted to share.

Choosing the version of me to speak for my heart, and the attitude that version uses when it speaks, makes it possible to impact those I cross paths with in powerful and life-transforming ways. The way I speak to people about anything displays my heart. Kind, gentle words or quick, sharp words can absolutely uplift or discourage the heart of another. Starting each morning with "I get to choose my attitude, I may as well choose a good one," makes life much sweeter on a daily basis, for myself and for everyone around me.

LESSONS LEARNED

1. I get to choose the version of me whom I want to speak for me.

2. The one thing that I control is my attitude. With God's grace, it can be a sweet one every single day.

3. If I allow a negative version of myself to speak for me, I run the risk of saying or reacting to things that I will just have to heal and recover from later.

COMPASS POINTS

1. What attitude best describes your day-to-day life experience? Explain.

2. What version of you would be your choice to be the one to tell your story? Why is this?

3. What version of the story would you prefer to be told? The dark and everything going wrong version, or the lessons learned and courageous version? How would life be different depending on which you chose?

If I plant diligence, I will reap a harvest of things accomplished and changes made. If I plant avoidance, I will reap the result of no change and things left undone. There is no way to bypass the end result of a lifestyle of avoidance.

From the Wilderness

To find clarity on the purposes and values that motivate us and make decisions all day long that demonstrate our commitment to those significant life principles, will be life altering.

From the Wilderness

22

I'D RATHER DO THIS THAN THAT

I have a book called *Life 101*. It's a good read with lots of great tidbits for creating positive habits for living. This book of life principles and lessons provides a road map for a successful life. One of the chapters in the book really caught my attention. It was titled, "You Can Have Anything You Want, But You Can't Have Everything You Want."

It's so true. There are only so many musical instruments one could learn. I could enjoy learning the guitar, or the piano, or the saxophone, but I would probably not have time to master all three. I could read two hundred books a year, but if I did I probably would not have time to learn any instrument at all. I could master a hobby, or the game of golf, but to do that I might not be able to learn to play any instrument or read 200 books a year either. Life comes down to prioritizing our commitments and the places we spend our time.

I could divide my time up between doing a hobby, golf, learning instruments and reading, but would have little or no time left for Gwen, for my children and grandchildren, or for my friends who mean a lot to me.

I have also discovered that when I try to do all the things I would like to do, I don't do any of them really well at all. And that is frustrating, because there are some very good things I would like to accomplish. It's not that I must make a choice between good things or bad things to occupy my time; it's that I'm often faced with making a choice between good things and other good things. Then what?

Sometimes the options are simply "I would like to do this, and I would like to do that." But what do I do when it comes down to choosing between a list of things I MUST do and a list of things I REALLY MUST do?" A "Must Do" list is more urgent and it can become overwhelming when there does not seem to be enough time in the day or week to make it all happen. Maybe you can also relate to the challenge I have faced sometimes where I just don't know how to manage all the important and urgent things coming at me all at one time.

Decisions regarding priorities require discipline. That is a commodity that many struggle with, some more than others. Discipline is a choice. I often think of a time when a friend was asked why he didn't want dessert at the end of a nice restaurant meal. His simple answer was, "I choose discipline." It is a statement I will not forget, and I refer to it many times when I have been faced with a choice that involves priorities. Would I rather eat that now and enjoy the taste sensations, or would I rather feel better later if I choose discipline? Would I rather spend my time doing what I want to do right now, or would I like the reward if I choose to spend my time taking care of the things that need to get done on a deadline? Would I rather do "this" or "that?" "I choose "discipline" can really help bring the right thing into focus for me.

But let's dig a little deeper. We are living in a world where we are constantly distracted. And maybe some of us would honestly admit that we even sometimes seek distraction. We may often avoid the things that require discipline and deep work. We may avoid good questions and the seeking of the truth because we fear it will require us to make harder, deeper choices, or change some part of our life that we are just not ready to give up. At least not just yet! Some fear they will be asked to do things that would take them out of their comfort zone, and who wouldn't rather settle for "comfortable?"

As we attended the *Choices* seminar, we processed many fabulous deep and challenging life principles. I remember saying to Gwen while we were there, "This isn't always easy, but it is always safe." Being asked to dig deeper and search for and face the truths in life that we would rather avoid is often the road less traveled. Safe does not always equate to easy, but experience teaches us that easy is not always the most rewarding. I find it invigorating to have my thinking challenged because it helps to ground my values, principles, and life purpose.

Avoiding discipline and rewarding decisions may even be the default for each of us at times. Like the fact that water takes the path of least resistance as it travels downhill, so our decisions often take the easy way. "I know I need to stop eating this, it's not good for me, and I plan to, but not today. One more is not going to hurt." Or, "I know that it would be better to get that task done, but right now I'd rather just chill and catch my breath, and I'll take care of that later." Some slide into those types of decisions on a regular basis with hardly any thought. Choosing discipline doesn't seem to be all that attractive sometimes. But we all know that little progress is made when life is lived without discipline.

I have come to realize that we may in fact be subconsciously seeking distraction, as that is a subtle way of avoiding something else that we do not want to do. The question we should always ask ourselves is, "What am I avoiding by not choosing discipline and instead just making this same default decision over and over again?"

Life is very full and chaotic at times. How often have we said yes to more commitments than is realistically possible? With little time to rest or pace ourselves, we weaken our resolve to take the actions necessary to live on purpose for the things that really matter. We just keep piling on the stuff we enjoy until we find ourselves overwhelmed.

In the Coaches Leadership training I participated in, they taught us about visually and mentally tying our ankle to a stake in the ground. That stake could represent anything we wanted it to be. By being tied to that stake, we could never drift far away and would always be held to our purpose and be reminded to return to its truth.

The stake could be the commitment to be a good spouse and when tied to that value, every decision made from that place would be about honoring that other person, and constantly choosing to live out the principles that create a happy relationship. That means that sometimes it would be necessary to say "no" to something I'd like to do right now, but discipline makes the right choice.

The stake might be the determination to be a positive and engaged parent. Once that decision is made, every decision that follows would be to enhance my parenting skills and to take the best interest in my children when making personal and family decisions. Again, it might mean saying no to my own interests sometimes, in order to honor the commitment I made to parenting my child.

Another stake might be the New Year's resolution to get back to good health, and when options are available for what to eat or how much rest or exercise is necessary, one would always choose the best way to enhance a healthy lifestyle because we are tied to that stake and the discipline that keeps us on task to accomplish that goal.

Many people don't have a clear purpose or "stake" guiding them on to any of the positive things they want to accomplish. We may have a general picture of what we want to achieve, and we may have a vague idea of the things required to get there, but the pace of life makes it seemingly impossible to focus on the multiple good things we know we should do. When the nebulous future is a bit hazy, choices made are often in the moment, and they are often decisions that tend to meet a very temporary desire. Those are the decisions that almost never bring about the desired outcome of the bigger life picture we want to create.

I could not count the number of decisions I have chosen to make that ignore and avoid the bigger picture of the things I want for my life. I totally understand and have demonstrated the reality of the lack of discipline at various times and circumstances. These decisions relate to the types of food I want to eat, things I want to experience, ways I want to spend my time, or opportunities to relax. The key word is avoid. In honest moments, I must admit that poor choices really come down to the issue of avoidance. We default into places that don't require thought or resistance, because we are avoiding making a disciplined decision about something. Why? Because there is always a payoff for everything we do. Why else would we do them? We avoid discipline because we like the payoff we receive from leaving things just as they are. It's comfortable there. We are in our safe zone.

Sometimes our comfort zones are actually prisons. I have learned that. We aren't really satisfied in our life, but neither are we energized enough to do anything about it, so we just stay there. Maybe one day we will do what we know we should, but not right now. It's always good to remember that life begins outside of our comfort zones. It's when we push ourselves, (I choose discipline) that we begin to really see rewarding results.

Someone recently said to me, "Whatever you plant, you will harvest." It's sort of a "yeah, no kidding," kind of statement, but a simple statement with a very profound reality to be aware of. If I plant diligence, I will reap a harvest of things accomplished and changes made. If I plant avoidance, I will reap the result of no change and things left undone. There is no way to bypass the end result of a lifestyle of avoidance.

For ten years, I spent a lot of time driving as I worked for the *Choices* program. I've seen every mile of the main highways of Alberta and Saskatchewan several times. I got into the habit of having the radio on for hours. I gravitated toward the talk shows. I would cover the miles listening to discussions on many topics, some invigorating and interesting, and many not worth the time spent. Over the course of time, I found it more rewarding to shut the radio off and just enjoy the silence, and my thoughts. Instead of having to do something to pass the hours and miles, I shifted to taking advantage of the time to let my mind rest. I had to ask myself, "Is there something I might be trying to avoid thinking about by needing to listen to talk shows hour after hour?"

I found that it was much more relaxing to just pay attention to the scenery around me and see what I would automatically notice without searching for anything. I have enjoyed the green freshness of Spring and the majestic Fall colors in many locations. I would look forward to certain drives at certain times of the year simply for what I knew I would see. Just letting my eyes take in that beauty was a refreshing thing. Focusing on radio talk shows would keep my mind occupied while I drove past and missed miles of outstanding scenic beauty. Yes, even on the prairies!!

With that in my mind, it was even more fulfilling when I added prayer and gratitude to the experience. I could thank God for eyes to see, and for His touch on the world that creates change season by season. It would often turn into a worship experience and I could find rest in the realization that Someone bigger than me oversees the world. I could make it very personal when I would reflect on the fact that if He was in charge of the world and could manage it well, He was also in charge of me and would make beautiful things there, too, if I would cooperate with Him.

Traveling in silence also simply gave me time to let my brain rest. Rather than the constant stimulation of input from a variety of people or music, I found that taking periods for silence was amazing in the peace it provided. I also learned that it was a way to think through and be better prepared for the events or details that would call for my attention at my destination. It was a time to sort my thoughts on many topics or issues I was dealing with. It was a quiet time to think about blessings I was grateful for in my life. I could remind myself of the gifts of God, and His work in my life, my family, and friends that I enjoyed. Silence became a friend as I found it to be a rewarding atmosphere to calm my heart and soul. But it came down to choosing discipline. I had a choice to do "this" or "that."

Back when I began my wilderness journey, I had a cell phone, but I did not have a smartphone. Those were not even on the market then. Phones were simply for calling people! Then came texting, and then it became a small computer. If you have one, you are fully aware of the power of that small box in your hand, pocket or purse, and the distraction that it can be.

I remember hearing a man say one time to "never go anywhere without a book. You never know when you will have to wait, or stand in line, and you can always do some reading." I still do that sometimes, but not as often anymore because I have my phone with me. It has books to read on it, but I find that I more often gravitate to email, internet news or topics, or too often, simply to the game apps, and spend a little time doing that while I wait. There are many ways to spend the hours in a day, and when I think of how many are spent on a screen, I am reminded that there are options and decisions to be made all the time. The ones I make may not be bad, but are they as empowering as I would like them to be? Do they keep me close to my stake and assist me in fulfilling my life purpose? I get to choose "This" or "That."

One time, I went through an exercise to develop a purpose statement or "stake" to guide my life. It is a statement that would enable me to embrace my commitment more easily as to where I want my focus to be as I interact with people, every day for the rest of my life. As I worked to find the right words, I considered the journey I had taken in life, and the wilderness I was in as a result. I determined that I would be committed to moving beyond the past and "finish well." I did not want my past to define the rest of my life.

But bigger than that, I wanted to be an example. I also wanted to be able to assist others, who might have had hard chapters in their lives, to see and know that they too could also finish well. I want them to clearly know that events and chapters in one's life do not mean the end of a rewarding life. The purpose statement, or stake, that I chose to define my life purpose would be that I would always commit myself to the work of "Encouraging Others to Finish Well."

I love having that stake to guide me as I visit with or coach people. When I mediate people, or even just chat with strangers, I watch to find ways to encourage everyone I speak to that it is always possible to make good things happen for the rest of the chapters in our lives and finish well.

When I have spent time in unproductive activity, I realize that I have not been living on purpose. We often make excuses for the times we spend playing or searching on our screens. We decide that we are tired, we've had a hard day, and we deserve a little numb-out time. It is true that we all need to rest; it makes us happier and healthier people. I have also learned that numbing my mind out on a phone app does not get me more of what I want, and may in fact be the opposite of rest. It does not make me a better or more productive person. In fact, the reality is that I may very well be avoiding something that I should be doing. We all need to check in with ourselves from time to time, or with the help of a friend or mentor, to determine the truth of what might really be going on behind the distractions.

We like to avoid our thoughts if we know that we have some things to deal with. Maybe we know we have things to make right. Possibly we have conversations that need to take place. Deep work, heart work, and rewarding work can all be avoided so easily by just excusing it with "I'm tired, I'll do this instead of that." And another day goes by.

How powerful it would be if each day we could wake up and live on task and purpose, all day long. What if when it came to deciding between "this" or "that", we would always choose the discipline of doing the things that will be most productive for what we want in life? All the time. Not in a grinding, driving, "I must do this whether I like it or not" type of way. To find clarity on the purposes and values that motivate us and make decisions all day long that demonstrate our commitment to those significant life principles, will be life altering. Forever!

Deep, rich fulfillment is available as we let our minds go to silent places and learn to visualize life with the values and the purpose we want to live by to motivate our lives. Then when it comes time to decide between "this" or "that" it would just automatically be easier and more rewarding, all the time.

LESSONS LEARNED

1. We only have so much time in a day, week, or lifetime. Momentary decisions made outside of the big picture of our lives may not be the ones that get us the results we are truly seeking.

2. There are many ways to numb out, and we can too easily come up with many good reasons (excuses?) for doing so. The check-in question is, "What might I be avoiding by choosing to do "this" right now?"

3. Silent times can be a friend. There are many creative things I can benefit from by shutting out the distraction of the world from time to time.

4. Finding a stake or purpose for living my life is a powerful way to keep focused on living the best life possible.

COMPASS POINTS

1. What might you be avoiding by the choices made on how to fill your time?

2. What is a simple, clear purpose statement, or stake, that defines where you want to focus your life?

3. If you must have the radio or music or television on all the time, what thoughts or places in your mind are you uncomfortable with?

4. When it comes to doing "this" or "that" how easy is it for you to "choose discipline?" Explain.

I'D RATHER DO THIS THAN THAT

NOTES FOR MY BACKPACK

Be accepting. Of everything. People's differences, their similarities, their choices, their personalities. Sometimes it takes a variety to make a good collection.
The same goes for people.

Colleen Hoover

You have to get along with people, but you also have to recognize that the strength of a team is different people with different perspectives and different personalities.

Steve Case

23

THE COLOR OF MY HEART

One of the most life-encompassing learning events I have experienced was to discover the *True Colors* personality profile. I was first introduced to it at the *Choices* program and became so amazed at the insights for life that it offered, that I took the training to become a certified facilitator. I have used what I discovered through *Colors* in every aspect of life and will continue to do so as long as I live.

We are wonderfully programmed in our beautiful minds to live life in patterns and value systems. Understanding the tendencies of those personalities can give us great insight into why we do what we do, or more accurately, why we do things the WAY we do them.

However, it also gives us understanding as to why others do what they do, and why they do it the way they choose to do it.

Colors is one of several personality profiles. Many attempts have been made to explain our way of experiencing and doing life. Some profile systems are more complex and detailed, but one of the many things I like about *Colors* is the simplicity and user-friendly value that it has. I'm not about to take you through a workshop here, but I want to quickly explain it.

Each of us has a blend of four basic personality styles within us. We possess all of them in varying degrees, but one or two that are dominant. That makes a certain way of life the automatic, go-to, path-of-least-resistance style that we normally end up choosing. It simply takes no thought or planning. It's as normal as breathing.

There are the Golds, who love to live with everything meticulously in order. Every item has a place, and every piece of paper, paper clip and sticky note is exactly where it belongs. If it's not, it can be a stressor. Life is lived by rules and guidelines, and much time is spent on attempting to figure out why others are not doing it the way they do it, which is of course the "right way". And the ONLY right way. There are no substitutes.

Gold personality people like to live by lists. Lists that catalogue information. Lists that organize the day, the week, the month, the next year. Some even have lists that catalogue all the lists they have. (Seriously!) Gold personality people often organize and hang their clothes by color or style, even socks and underwear drawers are done by color or whatever their organizational preference is. Drawers of items are never haphazard. The desk has nothing on it that does not need to be there. Time is important and late is never an option. Fifteen minutes early is about right on time. When you are going to meet with a Gold, be on time, but not too early because they have every minute scheduled until the meeting with you begins, and they don't want to be interrupted.

You get the picture. Gold personality people are very structured; life is planned into small packages of detail. Order is the natural flow of the day. Fun happens when the work is done, but for Golds the work is usually never done. The list is seldom finished. The best way for Golds to have fun is to put it on the list. Then lots of fun can take place because it's part of the scheduled plan.

We all need to have Gold in our lives. For some it is quick and natural, for others it is necessary to choose and focus on organizational skills from time to time just to keep on top of a never-ending list of things to do. When it is not the default personality style, it takes discipline and choice to get on top of clutter or disorganization.

Gold is not my first color, and my desk area can get very cluttered and messy looking at times. Finally, I get to the point where I know I must create some order. I then dig down and find all of that Gold trait within me and spend the time necessary to clean up, and once again organize my personal space. That's more of a task than a natural experience, but I can do it when it is necessary. We can all do it when it is necessary.

The Gold personality people keep the world on the rails. They provide the guidelines, rules and order necessary to accomplish tasks and details.

Blue personalities are those who think first and naturally in terms of relationships. How will what I am about to do feel good, make others feel good, and make existing relationships even stronger? Blue personality people are prone to think in feeling words, and decisions are often made, or not made, based on the emotions one has around those decisions. Hugs are natural. Spending time with loved ones or friends is crucial and never a chore. It is automatic and necessary. Blues are energized by being with other people.

The Blue personality is all about the heart work. Being close, comfortable, and cozy, both emotionally as well as physically, is the order of life. Blue people don't lie, but they may not tell the honest and full truth if it is believed that the full truth might hurt another person. It's all about safety and the care of hearts, all hearts. Everyone needs to be included. No one is to be excluded.

Blues cry easily, wear emotion easily and are not short on words. They like to explain things, and then explain it again so there is no question that it will be understood. If necessary, a third explanation would never hurt, just to make sure.

We need Blues to provide the healing and warmth in the world to balance out all the conflict that is present. Blues forgive easily, but have a hard time forgetting because the pain and emotion is what will always be remembered. Heart connection is crucial if life is to have meaning at all. There is much love for people and their wellbeing in the Blue heart.

The Green personality is summed up in the word "logic." Much time is spent thinking things through and processing information. All the information. And the green mind is never quite sure that they have all the information, so it's just not possible to make a decision, at least not yet. What if there is new information not yet known? That information might come today, in the next hour, and change everything. So, they wait, and think and process some more.

With the Green personality, there is much valuable information that comes from all the logic and processing that takes place. One can never go wrong to find out what a Green person thinks or decides and take their input seriously. They usually do a great job of working things out. It's just that it may take much longer than one had planned or has time for.

Green personality people are brilliant and deep. They have a struggle to tolerate speedy and quick decisions. Usually, if one asks a Green person for a commitment on something, the quick answer will almost always be "no". It's not that they don't want to do it, it's that they may feel they have not had time to think it all through yet as thoroughly as they would like, so a quick yes answer might be premature without adequate preparation. Given a little time, it's very possible the decision will be changed to a "yes" when there has been more time to process their thoughts and perspectives.

Green personality people tend not to show a lot of emotion. Their facial expression is often quite neutral. Their speech patterns don't carry a lot of feeling words. It can be hard to read a Green person by their body language alone. Their style of humor is often dry and quick and when understood they are a wonderful treasure to have in our world. As they say, "still waters run deep." That is often the case when observing the Green personality.

We need Green personalities in the world to give us invention, logic and ingenuity. Greens are not just thinking about how to do things, they are at the same time thinking about how to do it even better. That's just it! They are thinking! They are not ignoring us, but rather they are often just deep in thought! It's a wonderful and necessary personality trait.

And finally, there is the Orange personality. To sum it up in one word, the Orange personality lives a life of spontaneity. They are on a mission to make life one big adventure. Life is to be fun, so let's make it fun. Life is meant to use up every drip of adrenaline, so let's get on with it. It's the Orange personality types who more naturally take on the front-line professions such as paramedics, fire fighters, and police officers. They are typically the sky diver and the bungee jumper type. This does not mean that other personality types will not do these things, but the Orange personality does it quickly and without much hesitation. Adventure and excitement? Sure, let's do it! Can we start right now?

Orange types don't wait for the party to start, they start it. They don't wait for action; they are the action. Competition, loud laughter and living life in a light-hearted manner are all part of the game of life for the Orange personality. Like the Blues, Orange personalities don't lie, but they play with the truth for a different reason. To an Orange, there is no sense in telling a story if you can't make it a *really* good story. The facts by themselves might be a bit boring, so why not spice it up a little? Like the fisherman describing the size of the fish he caught, Orange types are known to exaggerate a few details along the way just to make the story more interesting. It's all about having few filters, being loud, and being fully alive and having fun!

We need Orange personalities in our lives just to help us not take life so seriously and to enjoy the wide, adventurous scope of how to see life. We need Orange people in our lives because they bring in the laughter, the adventure and the fun and creativity.

I'm hoping you see yourself in at least one of these brief descriptions. Remember, we are a combination of all four personalities, so don't be surprised if you relate to each one, but I'm guessing you will gravitate toward some more easily.

Why would I bother to tell you about all that? Because it was one of the biggest lessons I gained on my journey. This information really helped me sort out some of my wilderness questions and helped explain the reasons behind some of my life decisions and experiences. Our personality make-up never excuses our choices and way of processing life, but it can explain a lot of why we do some of the things we do. It has also helped me better relate to the people in my world. I now better understand others as they live life the way they do. It's as natural for them as can be.

I often say, dogs bark, cats meow, blues feel, greens think, oranges play, golds organize things. It's that automatic, and it makes life pretty simple. So, the lessons are many.

When I see a person acting a certain way, dressing a certain way, talking a certain way, I can't say for sure, but I begin to think about what their dominant color likely is. That immediately helps me to know how to relate to them as we talk together. As I said, it's user friendly and simple. It's much better to understand their actions, than to judge them. One lady said to me, "I discovered my husband is really not a jerk, he's just ____________." (I won't say what color she put in there.) It was eye opening and marriage changing for her to see her husband with new eyes and understanding. It's amazing what happens and how our insights open up when we learn how to recognize some of these things.

Every personality trait has a dark side as well as a strength. When life is stressful, the Gold personality can insist on being right because "this is what the rules say." They can dig in, be inflexible and begin to make judgments about those who do life other ways, which would, of course, in their eyes be the "wrong" way.

Greens can also get very focused on being right, but for a different reason. Since they are deep thinkers, and processors of information, they put in considerable time collecting data on any given topic. It seems obvious to them that others would never come to a better decision because they have not done the research or put in the time thinking about things in the same way. When there is tension or stress, there can be a sense of intolerance to others when logic is in charge.

Blues have a struggle with pleasing people and not making firm, convicted, and driven decisions because they constantly worry that they might hurt another person. It can become easier to go with the flow of what others want or think, rather than taking a stand and honoring one's conscience. When that happens, frustration can boil over, and Blues can lash out in their dark moments in hurtful ways towards others.

And, Orange personalities in the dark side may not take others seriously and can become a bit irresponsible and careless with their choices and words. Competition can turn into confrontation with little regard for others. Filters come off and things are said and done that many would like to have a second chance to do over.

As I learned about this more, I began to understand how my personality combination made me more open to making choices that might not be favorable in the long run. Knowing our personality types never excuse our choices and decisions, but they can certainly explain a lot of things. As I began to see where my own pitfalls in life would show up in my color combination, I was able to pause and make more rewarding choices.

The *Colors* information is a powerful learning tool. Spouses can understand and adjust to each other's way of doing life. Parents can see the patterns in children and adjust accordingly. Employers can look for people with strengths that enhance the position they are hiring for.

One of the greatest stories I heard was about a teacher who learned about *Colors* and decided to put it into play in her classroom. During the summer, she decorated her classroom in four styles, utilizing things that would be attractive to each personality. When school began in the Fall, she asked the students to spend a little time in each part of the room looking at the things that were there, and then go and stay in the one they would enjoy the most. In this simple way, she was able to have a little insight into her student's learning styles.

I have found that these personalities demonstrate themselves in almost every aspect of life. It even shows up in my relationship with God. As I thought about it, God knows how to relate to all of us in our personality styles.

The Gold personality is comfortable and secure in the guidelines He has laid out for us in the Bible. To boil it down to ten commandments, and then later summarize those ten into two commandments, gives the person who likes the security of rules to guide them a safe environment to work from. They see God as a God of order, which He is.

The Blue personality sees God in the context of relationship. They want to feel His presence and experience His interest in them personally. They search for the stories of how He loves people and all of mankind. The fact that His Son, Jesus, would leave Heaven and come to planet Earth to walk and live here with us is the kind of God this personality can easily love and appreciate.

The Orange personality loves the vast splendor and majesty of God. The heavens, the universe, the variety, the miracles He performs, all demonstrate how full, magnificent and powerful God is. He is a God of unlimited imagination in the way He created so many different trees, plants, creatures, and people. Having a relationship with a God like this is an adventure, just what the Orange personality lives and breathes for.

And for the Greens, God is a God of mystery. There is much to discover and figure out about Him. He shows enough of Himself to make Himself believable and real but hides enough of Himself to make Himself mysterious and Someone to search out. It's all very tantalizing and challenging for this personality.

God is the perfect combination of all these things. When He said, "Let us make man in Our image," and our individual personalities show up, we can know a little more about His beautiful character.

By understanding *Colors*, I discovered more about who God made me to be, and that tells me more about the life purpose He wants me to live out. I love all the lessons God is teaching me, and *Colors* taught me things that influence and help me understand so much of what I do and learn.

I have understood my wife, my daughters and my grandchildren better. I am not interested in seeking to make everyone fit into the mold I would choose for them, but I am much more curious about discovering the beautiful make-up of who God created everyone to be. I am much more understanding and willing to step over things about others that used to evoke a reaction out of me. Now that I can see and understand a bit why people do what they do, it's just easier to enjoy the differences in people whom I know and love.

LESSONS LEARNED

1. Understanding how God made and designed me provides deep insight into His plan for my life.

2. Understanding how God made and wired me provides deep insight into why I may be prone to make the choices I make. This can guide me into healthy choices that are free from regrets after I make them.

3. Learning about personalities has helped me know how to appreciate my family, friends, and the people I meet on a regular basis. I can understand and love each one in more meaningful ways.

COMPASS POINTS

1. From the brief explanation, which of the personality profiles do you resonate with? Why?

2. What insights do you gain about yourself from this discovery?

3. What insights do you gain about someone you are in a relationship with?

THE COLOR OF MY HEART

NOTES FOR MY BACKPACK

Good listening is designed to connect with others,
not to use their actions, responses,
or words against them.

From the Wilderness

It is hard to listen when you are talking,
or when you are thinking of a response.

Catherine Pulsifer

Don't listen with the intent of answering,
but with the intent of understanding.

Bobby Albert

24

EARS ARE FOR MORE THAN HOLDING UP OUR GLASSES

Aren't our ears an incredible blessing? There are so many ways to use them and enjoy the gift of hearing. There are the sounds of nature if we slow down long enough to notice. There is an amazing array of musical options that can entertain us. And what can top the sound of a child in innocent and hearty laughter?

We listen for our children in the night, one ear alert while we sleep. We love to hear their words as they try to form and mimic the sounds they hear. We laugh and cheer them on to "say it again," because we can't hear it enough. What a gift our ears are.

I believe in a creative Designer who made us with purpose and incredible detail. All the bones in our body grow, and some, such as those in our arms and legs, increase in size multiple times between birth and adulthood. And yet, I am told that the bones in the middle ear that affect our perception of sound must stay the same as at birth, and that if they did grow, we would go deaf. That is so amazing to me. What a miracle our ears and the gift of hearing are to us.

We have two ears and one mouth, obviously. I am sure that is not the most incredible fact you have heard today. I wonder sometimes though, what would change if it was the ratio that we would always communicate with. What would be different if we could learn to listen twice as much as we talk? Ears do a really great job of keeping our glasses in place! But that is just an added bonus on top of the amazing tool they are for connecting us to the people that matter most in our lives.

I have often thought of myself as well able to use words to create and enjoy humor with others. I have life experiences that I like to share with others when it is applicable. I have studied certain topics, and while I am not a specialist in any topic, I like to engage when I can share thoughts and perspectives. We all have words and ideas we can readily use as we communicate with others. All of this requires one tongue, and the discipline and filters needed to use it well.

Even more importantly, our ears are also a major factor in our communication skills. It goes without saying that we must listen deeply so that our words in response will be appropriate, helpful, and timed well. This requires the attentive use of our two ears to pay careful attention to the words and emotions of others. It's a skill. I simply assumed that my listening skills were good enough and never gave them much thought at all. When I was introduced to different levels of listening, I was amazed that there was a science to listening, and I realized I had much to learn. It was not good enough to just hear words. It was important to pay attention to so much more than just the words.

As I took mediation training, we were taught how to hear things that were not actually being articulated. However, it was during my introduction to life coaching that I began to learn how much of an art listening really is. I found out what could be very different when I learned to listen in levels, compared to what I had been more prone to do throughout my life in my interactions with others. More explicitly I realized I had been barely listening at all.

I learned about three levels of listening.

Level I is listening with my ears to the words, but being caught up in my own thoughts, responses, judgments and curiosity about what I am hearing. It is listening, but making the conversation a one-way interaction all in my direction. We are taking in the information, but keeping it all to sort for ourselves, using it for our sake, holding on to what we think is necessary for us, and rejecting the rest. The bottom line of Level I listening is thinking, "*What does this information mean to me?*"

Level l listening is not bad, and sometimes it is needed. We just need to recognize what it is, when to use it, and to stop using it when something else is required.

We need to use Level I listening skills when we are going to catch a flight. We need to make sure the tickets and passports are packed. We need to pay attention to how much time is needed at the airport to get through the security hoops before the boarding gate. We need to pay attention to flight numbers, announcements of gate changes, and find out if there are delays. This is Level I in its appropriate place.

If we go to order in a restaurant, we pay attention to the details of the menu, the price, and the ingredients if we have allergies. If we are in a doctor's office, we really need to use Level I listening because we need to pay attention to all the carefully detailed information. There are times we need this skill to be sharp.

Where Level I does not work is when we are listening to a friend or loved one. Maybe a spouse, a child, or a close friend has something on their heart that needs to be shared. This is where Level l can really be limiting in its scope.

For example, let's say a child comes home from school and says, "I've had it with school, I'm not going back! Ever!" Level I listening would respond by saying, "Of course you are going back. We've paid your tuition for the school year and you can't stop now. Besides, no one makes it in this world without an education. You don't want to be someone struggling their whole lives trying to make a living, do you? That's ridiculous. Go wash up, it's almost time for supper. And, while you're at it, maybe find a better attitude too."

Or, your spouse says to you, "I found out some really hard news today while I was at the doctor. We need to talk. I'm going for more tests tomorrow. She thinks it's urgent." Responding at Level I might look like, "Well, don't get ahead of yourself. You don't know what you don't know so don't borrow trouble. Sometimes these tests are wrong. Doctors make mistakes too, you know. Besides, you are healthy, you look great. I'm sure it will all be fine."

The listener is paying way more attention to their own feelings, opinions, and judgments than they are to the speaker's agenda. What is needed at a time like either of these scenarios is a more intentional way of listening.

Level I is noticeable when we interrupt and cut off the one who is speaking. Maybe we do it to be humorous, to make a quick point, or to react. Regardless, when we interrupt someone who is speaking, about anything, we are not listening well. When I learned this information, I was shocked at how often I was in a Level I place, and now I quickly notice others who do it without even being aware of what is happening. It can be very dishonoring to the speaker who just has a story to tell or a thought to share.

I invite you to pay attention when you are together with a group of people and watch how often someone who is speaking will be interrupted, sometimes in mid-sentence. They are left with their mouth open, ready to say the next word. The one who was speaking was not finished with their story or the point they were trying to make, but they must now wait for the one who interrupted them to finish making their own point or tell their story before they are able to complete the thought they were presenting. It happens far too often, and perfectly demonstrates Level I listening.

Level II listening changes the focus and puts it clearly on the speaker. The one who starts the conversation has the microphone, so to speak, and they are the one who sets the agenda. A good listener will focus on the one who is speaking and find out everything they can about the message being presented, and the reason that what they are sharing is important to them.

The listening now changes from a focus on me, my thoughts and my responses to the words I am hearing, to instead paying attention to what is happening for the other person. They are speaking, and Level II listening honors them and everything about what they are trying to say. Every question asked will open the door to that person's next words, thoughts and emotions. The goal is to create a place where the speaker can share safely and openly about what they are experiencing. Level II listening allows no room for judgment, opinion or even finding out my own curious details, which are all about Level I. At Level II the conversation is not about me anymore. It is all about the other person.

You can watch it happening from across a room. Someone will be leaning in listening intently. The words being shared are not animated or forceful. One person is talking and the other is oblivious to what is going on around them as the listening focus is clearly where it needs to be, on the speaker.

So back to the child coming home from school and announcing they are done with school forever. A person using Level II listening would take it in stride and say something like, "Wow. Sounds like someone has had a bad day. Here's a glass of lemonade, let's go out on the back deck and chat."

When they get there, the questions would be all about understanding the words and emotions that are driving the child at that time. "So, what's so bad about school that you are done and don't want to go back anymore?" A good Level II listener will then just follow the child's lead, use their words, and leave all judgments and opinions out of the conversation. Agreement is not important here, and neither is being right. What is important is the heart and story of the child in front of you. What is happening for them right now?

Some follow-up responses might be, "Can you tell me more about that?" "And what happened when those students were mean to you and your friends? That must have been horrible, and I can see why you would not want to go back there." Or, "Can you say more about why the teacher makes you not want to go back tomorrow?" Use their own words. If the child says, "I'm scared," ask them what they are scared about. If they use the word "terrified," use the word terrified. It's very helpful to use their exact language.

We attach importance and meaning to some words that someone else may not even notice. A word that resonates for me may be a word that may rarely be used by someone else. It's not that the word actually has a different meaning to be carefully defined, but it is important to use the words that resonate with the person we are listening to. So, if they say they were "terrified," they are giving a clue to the fact that it is an important word to them. If we say back, "What made you so afraid?" we may be using a word that doesn't have much "punch" for them, and by doing so we take away the impact of the discussion.

When we focus in on the words others are using, we are demonstrating that we truly are listening well and paying attention to their hearts.

As you continue talking with the child who does not want to go back to school tomorrow, in your mind you may be making a note to talk to someone about the bullying, or about the atmosphere in the classroom, but that is not part of this discussion. Level II listening goes to the heart of the child in the moment and pays close attention to what is happening there. The focus is, and always remains about what is happening with the speaker.

Of course, as the parent, you at some time will want to explore options and solutions to the issue, but that is not until the child has had the opportunity to open their heart and words and spill it all out. It may take only a few minutes and sometimes maybe longer, but the solution discussion is best to remain on hold until that has happened.

If your spouse comes in and tells you he/she had a bad appointment at the doctor, two things are important. What did the doctor say, and what is that spouse experiencing as a result of the appointment? What are their emotions? Finding out what the doctor said is simply to understand the context of what the speaker will say next. It's not about satisfying all my curious questions about the details and it has nothing at all to do with trying to talk them down out of their fear. This is not a time for advice or opinion or playing amateur medical professional. All of that is Level I listening. If they are really frightened, let them express it, and then go on to explore that fear. Stay with them. Get them to say more. The attention is purposely placed on the other person. This is their story and their time, and the goal is to make sure we give that to them.

I have often made the mistake of listening in Level 1 when I should have been giving the speaker a better spotlight. I have allowed my thoughts, opinions and judgments to cloud the conversation and what I should be listening to. The end results of those conversations are never what I, or they, want or hope them to be. There may not be any argument, but neither is there a deep or satisfying result.

And then, I also learned about Level III listening. This is where we pay attention to the atmosphere around the conversation. It's about things we observe with our senses along with the words that we are hearing with our ears. What do we see, feel and hear outside of the speaker's words? Is there tension? Are there tears? Are the tears barely rolling down the cheek or are the tears dripping off the chin? Is there laughter? Is the voice raised and shouting? Are the eyes darting and afraid? Does the tone of voice change, and how?

The goal is not to make assumptions or judgments about what is observed, but to use those as clues as to what to explore or ask next. A gentle, "I notice the tears. Tell me about the tears," is much different than "So now you're crying, again! You always cry those crocodile tears just to get your own way." Good listening is designed to connect with others, not to use their actions, responses or words against them.

I continue to learn about listening and its power. I wish I could say that because I have learned more about listening that I do it right all the time. There are times I listen and immediately go to Level 1 and form an opinion or judgment. Sometimes I cut in or plan my response. When I recognize I have done that yet once again it helps me to quickly shift to a much deeper listening focus. To listen carefully to someone in Level II is a lesson I am still practicing, and when I do it well, it is very rewarding.

However, there is a much deeper lesson to everything I have just said. I have learned that often we listen to God at different levels too.

God's purpose for all of us is to have a personal, loving, and restorative relationship with Him. He wants His presence and His wisdom to be rewarding to us in our everyday lives. His purpose is always good.

As I think about my life, I realize that sometimes however, when He teaches or calls to me through something I am reading, I am listening at Level I. At those times I am more prone to form an opinion about what His message might mean for me rather than simply take in the message itself. I get caught up in thinking about how it's going to impact me rather than listening to His heart and seeking to understand what He is really trying to say to me. I think of times where I reasoned with Him, philosophically responding rather than obediently responding. I have obviously, at times, made choices where I was ignoring His advice, listening only at Level I to Him. I could hear His voice but I was only thinking about me.

If a meaningful and rich relationship with God is important to me, I will apply the levels of listening to my relationship with Him. I will always realize the importance of listening deeply when He speaks to me. I will choose to fully explore what the depth and the purpose of His words are to me. I want to understand His heart and why His words and message to me matters to Him.

I think back to my hero, Moses, who I told you about in the introduction. After he had been in the wilderness for forty years, God came to him in a burning bush. You can read about it in the Book of Exodus in the Bible, in chapters three and four. After explaining why God wanted his attention, God summarized His message when He commanded, "Now go, for I am sending you to Pharaoh. You will lead my people, the Israelites, out of Egypt." Exodus 3:4 NLT

The next several verses cover four different excuses that Moses had for God as to why this could not be possible. Moses was listening at Level l. It was not an attempt to understand God or to find out

God's heart. He actually in the end pleaded, "Lord, please! Send someone else." Exodus 4:13 NLT

I'm not sure of everything going on in Moses' mind, but I could guess that he was simply afraid to set his foot back into the land of Egypt, even after forty years. It seems he was thinking totally about himself as he made up all the excuses and finally just pleaded with God to leave him out of it.

Had he been listening at a deeper level, he would have been more curious about what God was thinking, and why He had chosen him for this great task. He could say, "I'm afraid. I left Egypt afraid and I still am. Could you tell me more about this? Why me? Do I have to do this alone, or will you be with me?" He could have searched deeply to know exactly what God would tell him about the plan, but God was so busy answering his excuses that they never did get to that.

I compare Moses' conversation with God to that of Mary, the mother of Jesus, when the angel came to her and said that she was going to give birth to a very special baby who was going to be "called the Son of the Most High." Luke 1:32 (NLT)

Mary asked the angel, "But how can I have a baby? I am a virgin." After the angel answered about the miraculous conception that would happen in Mary, she simply responded, "I am the Lord's servant, and I am willing to accept whatever he wants. May everything you have said come true." Luke 1:34, and 38.

Level III listening to God is simply the work of looking around us and paying attention to what we see. There are so many things in the universe itself that remind us there must be a designer.

If we look at a flower garden that is perfectly manicured with every blade of grass the same height, we know for sure that there is a gardener nearby somewhere. There are so many things that give reason for us to reflect in awe and wonder. The beauty in the mountains, in the prairies, in the ocean and in the desert. The mystery of space, stars and planets. The science of understanding the earth's relationship to the sun and how they are perfectly placed in relationship to one another. And there is the amazing mystery of DNA.

There is the sparkling love between two hearts as people find attraction and romance, the beautiful miracle of birth and the smile of an infant. Then the wonder and curiosity of a child as they program their "mental computers".

It is hard to verbalize the peace that comes to a person when they discover God and find His purpose for them. Lives are changed from anger to peace. From addiction to freedom. From fear to courage. These are things we observe in the space around us as we watch God work.

I am a student of personal growth. I love to learn skills that help me be a better person and be skilled at how to interact with people every day. I want to be a good listener, and I have shared a few of the listening skills that can help make that happen. Listening well to others opens a whole new level of relationship with amazing rewards of connection and intimacy.

I am also a student of spiritual growth. I have discovered that learning to listen to God correctly is even more important than listening to others, but can be done with the same skills.

So, I'm glad we have ears. They do a great job of holding up our glasses. They also have the amazing ability to make our lives and the world a much happier and well-connected place. I want to use mine well for that purpose more than anything else.

LESSONS LEARNED

1. Good listening is not automatic, but there are tools we can learn that will forever change our relationship to people and how we honor them.

2. Making the effort to think about others as we listen, rather than ourselves, opens the door to a deeper connection that we may not have ever experienced before.

3. When we learn to listen to God differently, we are able to see Him with very different eyes and understand why it is that He guides us the way He does.

4. Learning to pay attention to the space and atmosphere around us can teach us many things that words will never be able to.

COMPASS POINTS

1. In what ways do you demonstrate that you listen at Level I?

2. In what ways do you demonstrate that you listen at Level II?

3. As you evaluate the differences, which level brings more satisfactory results in your interactions, and why?

4. What would change in your relationships if Level II listening became more of an automatic habit?

5. Do you have someone in your life who listens to your heart with a Level II skill? What do they do that lets you know this?

6. What would change in your life if you paid more attention to the wonderment of all the Level III, unspoken experiences in the world around us?

NOTES FOR MY BACKPACK

Because something was important and precious at one time
way back when, does not mean it's junk now.
It's just part of a different story in my life than
the one I'm living today.

From the Wilderness

What are you pretending not to know?

From the Wilderness

What other things might I be avoiding that are
cluttering up my mind and taking up my
emotional space and energy?

From the Wilderness

25

NOT ALL THE BOXES ARE UNDER THE STAIRS

At the time that I resigned from my life as a pastor, I had many personal things in my office that needed to be moved to my home. It took several boxes to pack up all my belongings and required a couple of pickup truck loads to move them and form a stack in my basement. Eventually I made room under the stairway where I tucked them away. The plan was to sort through them at another time when I had the emotional energy to do so. The papers and materials in those boxes were tokens of my life as I had known it for almost 24 years. There were certificates, pictures, keepsakes, files and knickknacks that represented many events and memories. It was a collection of items that had meaning only to me, but in my mind, they were treasures. That was in May of 2000.

Seven years later, in the summer of 2007, a classmate and I were participating in an assignment as part of my life coaching training. We were on the telephone, and I had never met her in person. I have forgotten the topic we were discussing, but somewhere in the conversation I mentioned those boxes under the stairs. I spoke about them as memories that had been stored away for seven years already, and that I was obviously avoiding the task of digging into them, because they represented such a deep, personal journey. I acknowledged that I needed to go through them but I was hesitant because of the emotional response it would likely bring up for me as I once again handled these items of a life that was so precious, and that I had recklessly destroyed.

At some point in the conversation, being a good coach, she asked a very significant and thought-provoking question. This was another one of the many I had been asked through the years, some of which I have shared in this book. She said, "Bill, not all the boxes are under the stairs. What else in your life might you be avoiding?" I can remember that question like it was spoken yesterday.

I interpreted it to mean, "Are there any "boxes" in your mind, cluttering up your emotional space, stealing your energy that you need to step into and deal with so that you are able to experience the freedom that would come from doing that?"

Those boxes remained tucked away under the stairs for two decades, until April of 2020! When the Covid pandemic hit planet Earth and we were all staying home except to go out for necessities, I had a lot of time on my hands, in my house. I decided it was time to head under the stairs and do the work that I had been avoiding for the last twenty years. It was time. I had put it off long enough, and the day to change that had arrived.

It took three days to go through all the boxes. To my surprise, much of the material was simply ready to be trashed or recycled. I discovered that many things that I had considered treasures at one point, were actually not even relevant anymore. They were all part of another story, not the present one. It was easier, with the amount of time delay, to let these items go and say good-by to them as I realized that possessions that had once been treasures were now simply sweet memories. So many new things were now taking the focus of my attention. There were very few tangible items that needed to be saved or allowed to take up space under the stairs any longer.

In a conversation I was having recently with a peer group, I mentioned all the "stuff" I had around my house that I didn't really know what to do with. I mentioned how I had collected many "treasures" at different times for different reasons, and that even though those reasons didn't exist anymore, it was hard to just throw things out. For example, I told them that I have a rock, that is a few pounds in weight, that's been on a shelf for thirty-eight years. It is jagged and pointed on one end. I picked it up in 1984 from a building site in Saint John, New Brunswick, where a basement for a new home was being blasted by dynamite out of rocky ground. I was going to preach a sermon on the story in the bible where an adulterous woman had been brought to Jesus for judgment, and the people reminded Him that the law said she should be stoned. He turned the tables on them when he told the people to go ahead and stone her. He made one rule, that the one who had no sin could cast the first stone at her.

This rock was a perfect illustration for that sermon. I wanted to use it as a visual reminder that none of us have the right to cast the first stone on anyone, because we are all broken and sinful in some way. I kept the rock and moved it along from office to office whenever we transferred to different churches. At least four more times in my life I have preached a similar sermon and used that same stone to illustrate "The First Stone," and that if we are without sin, we can freely throw it at another who is sinning. It's also been a personal reminder to me, as I notice it on my shelf, to not be harsh and judgmental toward others. Now. I'm retired and may not ever preach that story again. The stone is taking up space on a shelf. I have many other things such as that stacked in closets and boxes throughout our house.

In this recent conversation, as I spoke about this rock, I said I didn't want to keep moving it with me forever, but I had already packed it around with me for 36 years. It didn't seem right to just toss it over a bank somewhere. Someone suggested, "It's not trash, it simply was part of another story at another time." That thought reminded me about my boxes under the stairs story. Because something was important and precious at one time way back when, does not mean it's junk now. It's just part of a different story in my life than the one I'm living today. It may have been relevant at another time, but it isn't part of this story.

Through those discussions I learned another lesson. It is a lesson that has three layers.

Over time we can accumulate more keepsakes and articles of memorabilia than we can manage. Pretty soon we are unable to keep track of it all, but hesitate to throw anything away because it represents a memory or a time in life that we cherish. By remembering that our lives are a series of stories, we can honor the items of other stories much easier. Putting things into the context of the story in which they fit helps to minimize the clutter of our current life story.

Recognizing this will be helpful for me in days ahead as I sort through closets and boxes kept from years gone by. It will be easier to deal with tangible boxes full of items that are taking up physical space in my house and garage. These are part of a sweet, real, but other story.

However, there are deeper questions that remain to be answered. My coaching classmate had asked, "Not all the boxes are under the stairs. What else in your life are you avoiding?" I needed to stop and consider what other things might I be avoiding that are cluttering up my mind and taking up my emotional space and energy?

I love good questions. I love asking them, and I love it when people ask them of me. There are many life situations, habits, addictions or lifestyles that people are experiencing which are not satisfying. They may not know what to do in order to change their circumstances, so instead of adjusting, it's easier to just pretend that everything is okay or as good as it's going to get.

We might pretend that relationships are alive and well when we know deep inside that they are dull and coasting. Or even worse.

Many people pretend that they like the job they are in because they don't have the courage to quit and look for something else. Others pretend that the pain in their body is really nothing to worry about, and they are sure it will go away and everything will be just fine.

How often do people pretend that they are peaceful and happy when they know that they are unsettled and not taking care of matters that really should not be ignored?

And, on another level yet, some people have nagging questions about God but don't know how to sort them out or take the time to find answers. They may not even know where to start if they wanted to. Like the boxes under the stairs, these questions can be ignored for a time, but they never go away. Until they are addressed, the questions pop up at different times, even unexpectedly. A friend dies, and suddenly we wonder again about what really happens to a person after we die. A tragedy happens somewhere in the world that catches our attention, and once again we are confronted with the question about how there can be a loving and powerful God and such ugly events at the same time.

Then there is the whole question of being good enough. Is there really a heaven, and if so, how do I get there? Many people spend their whole lives in fear because they believe in a version of God that says they must jump through many hoops in order to be good enough to please Him when they stand before Him. Many are often never sure if they measure up. I have met many people who struggle with that nagging doubt. They realize they are human, failing sometimes, and become quite discouraged. For a variety of reasons, instead of digging in and searching to find out the answers to what a satisfying relationship with God looks like, some find it easier to just put those questions on the back burner for now. And like the boxes under the stairs, the questions are not dealt with for maybe years at a time.

"The Boxes Under the Stairs" is a metaphor for the question of when to deal with the unfinished business in our minds that should not be ignored any longer.

We need to constantly check in with ourselves and ask, "What am I avoiding? What am I pretending not to know? Who do I need to forgive and reconcile with? Who do I owe money or an apology to that I need to settle and clear up? What do I need to let go of? Why do I keep pulling old useless "baggage" along behind me that constantly slows me down by taking up precious emotional energy?"

A question I heard once asked, "Why do you let that person live rent free in your head?" Living rent free means someone occupies space, uses lights, heat, water and causes wear and tear on the place without ever paying anything in return. Living rent free in my head allows a person or situation to occupy my thoughts, emotions, and energy without giving any joy or satisfaction in return. We would do well if we would just let go of memories, regrets, bitterness and anger that are not uplifting or positive. It's important to remember that some things were simply all part of another story, one that we are not living any more. It really produces a lot of freedom to let that story stay back in the past in its rightful place.

My coach friend was right. Not all the boxes are under the stairs. I finally unpacked them and created a lot of space. I've also learned to unpack some questions, thoughts and reminders that have taken up emotional energy for far too long. I now experience the freedom that comes when I let go of things that once caused pain in my heart and mind.

What is taking up space in your heart or mind or soul that needs to be unpacked, dealt with and settled so the freedom and emotional space you deserve can open up and be free for you to use?

LESSONS LEARNED

1. Not all things from my past, keepsakes, or tangible memorabilia, need to be carried forever in order to honor them.

2. It is important to acknowledge the things we are avoiding and deal with them appropriately.

3. What do we need to change, who do we need to forgive? What are we pretending not to know?

COMPASS POINTS

1. What areas of your life might you be avoiding even though there are things there to deal with?

2. What things or memories are you keeping that are actually part of an old story and not part of the one you are living in now and need to be let go of?

3. What would change for you if all the "boxes" in your life were gone through and finally sorted out?

4. What are you pretending not to know?

NOT ALL THE BOXES ARE UNDER THE STAIRS

NOTES FOR MY BACKPACK

Life is never made unbearable by circumstances,
but only by lack of meaning and purpose.

Viktor Frankl

Right is right even if no one is doing it;
wrong is wrong even if everyone is doing it.

Augustine

Since God has revealed how His and my story blend together, and that I was created with meaning and purpose, it seems natural that I am not just here for a blip in time, and then nothing more.

From the Wilderness

26

MY GUIDING COMPASS

Beginning any journey requires some thought, planning and preparation. We need to prepare food and snacks for the trip, as well as make sure the gas tank is full. Time is required to pack the suitcase and all the extra items that will be needed on the trip and at the destination. And, beyond all that, we need to be aware if we need directional information and maps to make sure we will arrive where we want to go.

Sometimes we set out for a leisurely, site-seeing drive, with no particular destination in mind. However, there are other times when the destination is specific and the territory is unfamiliar. Paper maps used to be the state-of-the-art tool to keep us from getting lost. Today, there are electronic GPS devices. In recent years, these devices have become common tools on any smartphone device, and I use mine on a regular basis.

When GPS tools first came out, they were specific devices for navigation purposes only. We once traveled to Europe, and with the assistance of a small GPS device the size of a cell phone, we were able to easily navigate our way through cities, where on my own I would have had absolutely no idea how to find my way around. Without missing a street or a turn, that GPS device guided us through Stockholm, Berlin, Frankfurt, Amsterdam, and Oslo as well as many other places in between. I easily navigated thousands of freeway miles and hours of travel in Sweden, Germany, Holland, Denmark, and Norway, places I had never been to before. Having the electronic voice in the little box telling me to prepare to turn left in one half kilometer or stay in the second from the left-hand lane as I traveled made it as easy as if I was driving on my own street next to my house.

However, we clearly found out what happens when we did not have the voice to guide us for a time. After checking into a hotel in Oslo, Norway, we took our luggage to our room, and then decided to go back to the lobby to find an ATM machine to get some local currency. It turned out that there was no cash machine in the hotel, but the clerk at the desk said as she pointed, "There is one in the strip mall just up the street. You can't miss it." The GPS device was upstairs in our room. We debated on taking the time to go to get it and decided that we could surely find that strip mall. After all, it was "just up the street." "Let's just go without it! How hard can this be!"

I'm not sure how we missed it, but we didn't find a strip mall of any kind, let alone a cash machine. We decided to drive on just a little further and see if we maybe had not gone far enough and our destination was still ahead of us. We would also watch for a gas station or a bank that might have what we were looking for.

When we arrived in the city earlier that day, we had discovered that Oslo is a fascinating city with miles and miles of tunnels. It was incredible to experience intersecting tunnels, freeways merging with other freeways and everything that goes with that, all underground! Sixty to seventy miles an hour with no sunlight, and nothing to orient us as to whether we were going east or west. All we could do was just keep up with the flow of traffic and watch for exit signs. As we went a little further up the street in search of that ATM, suddenly, with no way to turn around, we had no choice but to head into one of those tunnels. Thankfully, it was not one of the long ones and we soon were out and able to exit onto a side street. Now, we really did not know where we were, or what streets we needed to take to get back. To make matters worse, believe it or not, we could not remember the exact name of the hotel we were staying in. This was a country we were not familiar with, and it was not a Best Western or a Holiday Inn we were looking for. And, we could clearly picture that GPS device upstairs in the hotel room! Do you see any problems shaping up here?

We stopped at two gas stations, but even though we could all speak English, the bewildered clerks were not able to help us much because we could not exactly explain where we wanted to go. We could only point in the general direction and ask how we might get back. They did their best. Oh, if only we had taken the "electronic lady" in the GPS device with us, we would be fine. But we had set it down and left it behind!

We found a cash machine, and then kept driving, and guessing, and hoping as we followed our best instincts. Finally, we saw a familiar landmark and exclaimed, "That is close to the hotel!" Within a few more minutes we were back in our room, hugging that little machine. In total, it had taken less than an hour, but we vowed that we would never, ever again let "her" be out of our sight.

In the wilderness journey I have told you about, I experienced a lot of "travel" that was spent doing a lot of searching. It was territory I had never navigated before. I was determined to not let my life be remembered by the scandal I had created, or the failure I had demonstrated.

Like entering that tunnel in Norway, I had not planned this journey, but I knew that it was not the place I wanted to remain. I wanted to find my way back home to the peaceful, respectful place of integrity that I had once known. I was in very unfamiliar and undesirable territory, searching for reference points to direct me back home.

We learn nothing in a vacuum. There is always a setting for the learning we experience. Throughout my life I have had an internal GPS that guides me, as long as I remember to take it with me. Then, there came a time when I trusted my own sense of direction and set it down. I believed I could navigate my own way. That is when I completely lost my way.

Scattered throughout the pages of this book are small references to my internal GPS. I want to succinctly summarize the points that form the compass that I choose to use to guide my heart.

Wherever we are on the journey of life, there are four questions that we seek answers to. I am sure that you know them and have asked them in some form or another, but they can be boiled down for us as follows:

1. Origin: Where do I come from?
2. Meaning: What is life's purpose? What is my purpose for being here?
3. Morality: How do I determine and differentiate between good or evil/right or wrong?
4. Destiny: What happens to a human being when he or she dies? Is this all there is?

A life lived in perfect satisfaction, or a life lived with continued interruption and emotional chaos, will in some way ponder these questions at some point. The human heart beats the same regardless of gender, race, culture or status. The answers we accept form the life compass that we live through and choose to be guided by.

I believe the Bible addresses all four of these questions. The answers I find there form the compass that I want to follow.

Erwin McManus is a pastor from California who has written several thought-provoking books. I was privileged to attend a live presentation he gave one day and wrote down one of his statements that I thought was worth remembering. He said, "If you can trust what the Bible says about man, you can trust what the Bible says about God." When I consider what the Bible says about the experience of mankind, and then compare that to my life, I can agree that the Bible has a very clear picture of the human condition.

The Bible explains that all things were created by the hand of this powerful God who is able to create life just by speaking the words. A Designer with unlimited power is easily able to form a body, put life into it, and turn that life switch on. That is my origin. I didn't just appear.

Believing that I came to life at the hand of a Designer then implies that there is a distinct purpose to my life. A reason for me to be here. I have never made anything without there being a reason for creating it. A Designer has a reason for doing what He does, too, and I do well to search that out in answer to the "Why am I here?" question. Finding purpose and meaning to everyday life provides reason and energy for getting up in the morning.

The third big life question is what determines good and evil, or right and wrong? How do I even know that my decisions are good or bad? Is my philosophy of life the final answer to everything? Do I get to determine what is good or bad all on my own? Does the final distinction rest with me?

I have enjoyed a story that illustrates this well. The captain of a ship on the dark water at night, sees a light in the distance and it looks like they are on a collision course. The captain of the ship sends a signal to whoever is represented by the light ahead and directs that ship to change its course ten degrees to the North. Quickly the light ahead signals back and says, "You change your course ten degrees to the South."

The captain is reactive and quickly signals back, "This is Captain Jones, you turn your ship ten degrees to the North." The immediate reply reads, "This is Private Smith, you turn your ship ten degrees to the South."

The captain becomes angry and quickly responds, "This is a battleship, and we are loaded and able to fire at will. You turn your ship ten degrees to the North." The quick reply ended the discussion when the message read, "This is a lighthouse. You turn your ship ten degrees to the South."

I could try to navigate my own life and decide what is good or evil, but to me, the Bible acts as a lighthouse that has the final say regardless of whatever I might decide. When I trusted my own navigation skills for life and did not pay attention to what I had trusted for so long, I found out how foolish that was. By ignoring God's measure of right and wrong for a time and setting my own compass I became completely disoriented and experienced a horrific loss of integrity, dignity and peace.

And for the fourth big life question about destiny, I have a very bright confidence of what the future looks like. Since God has revealed how His story and my story blend together, and that I was created with meaning and purpose, it seems natural that I am not just here for a short blip in time and then nothing more. We are here to enjoy the journey, but also to have a final, majestic destiny. I believe that death is real, but only temporary, and that tombstones do not mark our final resting place. A God of unlimited power has the final word on death and it is no match for Him. God has an eternal goal in mind for us that is perfect, right, and good, and is permanent for me and all who want to be there.

This book is about the journey into the wilderness that I took, when for a time, I did not pay close attention to these principles that make up that life compass. Like leaving the one device in the hotel room that would guide me while I went looking for an ATM machine in Oslo, I, for a time, set my personal life compass down and made turns that took me places I never planned to go. I attempted to convince myself I would be just fine and could navigate on my own. I thought I knew the way and my GPS would not be necessary. I tragically found out how wrong I was.

It proved experientially fatal to me to ignore that the Designer of my life had a purpose for me. That purpose included my witness to a fulfilled life when I maintained a commitment to honesty and integrity. It included the need to pay attention to right and wrong. If I had stayed close to paying attention to the design and desire that He had on my life I would have never taken the wilderness detour. When I set my personal GPS compass down I paid a very significant price.

When I was a seminary student in 1980, my personal faith in these beliefs was challenged in a very real way. For two years, I lived in a setting of young and amateur scholars where it is normal to rub shoulders with those who like to ask challenging theological questions. These questions were not always asked to find answers necessarily, but were sometimes asked to insinuate that the usual or accepted answer was not adequate. Often these questions were asked as an invitation to debate to see who was "right!" These types of discussions were going on constantly. They were full of emotion and passion. I began to ponder about some of the things I had heard and began to question some of my own thoughts. As a result, I became a bit disoriented.

That led me to a very confusing and unsettling time where I really began to wonder if in fact I had simply adopted the beliefs of my parents without checking to see if they were valid. Was there any good evidence and reason to actually trust them?

One day, probably at the lowest moment of my struggle about all of this, I distinctly remember laying on my back on my bedroom floor staring at the ceiling. I was speaking out loud to Gwen and questioning whether I had just been taught a series of fables all my life. As I spoke my thoughts out loud, I realized that I needed to do something about this. I got up off that floor and made myself a promise. I determined I was going to search, and not stop searching, until I found out the answers to my questions, once and for all. I would search for my own evidence and a personal reason for my beliefs, if they were in fact there to be found.

I was already taking a full load of classes that kept me busy, but I found the personal time to study, dig and verify the compass points that had guided me up until then. I probed deeply, asked the "why" questions, and checked the strength and depth of the foundation of my belief system. Over the next few weeks, something very powerful began to take shape for me. It was this process that moved me from believing things because my parents taught them to me, to grasping on to that compass as my own. I now believed the very same things, but I believed them because I had checked them out for myself, and they were real and deeply personal to me.

That was many years ago. From then on, and for the rest of my life, these points are still the convictions that I personally hold on to. I paid a heavy price for not always letting them be the lighthouse to guide me, but I have returned to them and I would rather die than give them up again. This gracious God I believe in makes it possible to pick up the tattered pieces of broken hearts and make them into a mosaic that is fascinating in its new design, and is stronger than ever. As you have read about the lessons gathered along my journey, ultimately it was returning to these convictions that kept me oriented in the dark and dry times. Without them I don't know if I would be where I am today. As I began to let them have their rightful place in my life once again, they kept me safe and on track through the wilderness and made it possible for me to find my way home and finish well.

LESSONS LEARNED

1. All compass points for guidance in life must be personal and cannot be passed down from parents or teachers.

2. A compass is of absolutely no value if it is ignored or set aside.

3. Lessons in life are learned in the context of our belief systems. If my belief system is ignored, there is no place for the lessons of life to find meaning.

4. A GPS left upstairs is a recipe for regrets! So is letting go of the life principles that guide my life.

COMPASS POINTS

1. What are the compass points that give you reference for the big questions of life?

2. Where did you get your compass? What makes it a true and safe guide to follow?

NOTES FOR MY BACKPACK

I realized that I knew a lot about Jesus, but I was now going to find out if I knew Jesus personally. It's a very different thing to know about someone than to personally and intimately know that person.

From the Wilderness

We need help. We need someone other than one of us. Someone with more power, and with a tender compassion for the human condition. We will never be able to get out of this reality that we are in without help.

From the Wilderness

27

GETTING TO KNOW JESUS AGAIN FOR THE FIRST TIME

There has never been a time when I have not known the name Jesus. Before I was old enough to remember, my parents were taking me to church. I don't recall the first time I was at church, but it was a part of life for me and my family. I learned to pray as a child. I learned to sing songs about Jesus, and I'm sure that "Jesus Loves Me, This I Know," was one of the first ones they taught me.

My mother loved to read, and stories were a part of an almost daily, and for sure, weekly routine. We had a set of ten Bible Story books that told the story of the Bible from beginning to end. Complete with art on every page, it was a set of books that fascinated me. When she finished reading the last chapter of the last book, I wanted her to start again. I knew which parts were my favorites, and patiently waited through the parts that were a bit boring to me so we could get to the best parts. As soon as I was able to, I read the stories myself. The adventures of the Bible characters are still etched in my memory because of those childhood stories.

As I grew older, I developed a deeper knowledge of Jesus. I read more mature writings about Him, about what He did, and why His life and death were so important to me and to all mankind. I attended schools where Bible classes were a part of the annual curriculum along with "readin', writin' and 'rithmatic." Different parts and themes of the Bible were presented to give a variety of teaching points, and it was designed to give a broad picture and understanding of Scripture. Attending church was a way of life, and that, along with school and the stories at home gave me a great Biblical foundation for my future work as a pastor.

When I graduated from High School, I decided that I would register for college in the fall and study theology. However, when the summer was over and I signed up for college classes, I was not convinced that theology was truly my field of interest, so I registered for a broad schedule of general topics. I took one semester, and then decided to drop out for a semester. The next fall, I again registered, but for basic, general classes, still not sure what I wanted to focus on.

In September of 1974, I moved to La Sierra University in Riverside, California. I was drawn there because my girlfriend (Gwen) was going there that fall to begin nursing school. She was clearly set on her career goals, but I was still floundering a bit on mine. We began the adventure of living a university dormitory lifestyle in Southern California. That part was easy, but choosing an education career path, not so much. When it came time to register, I said, "I would like to become a Bible Teacher." I was told there was no such program, but that if I registered for education and took religion as a minor degree, I would likely be able to find a position to teach the Bible in a church academy somewhere.

The next step was to decide what my major emphasis in education would be. I had no clue. I decided that since I was from Canada, and had taken a lot of French classes which I found not too difficult, why not major in French?! That started me into a year of French and education classes with a plan to, at some point, go to Paris for 10 weeks on a total immersion program. It was not a life-long dream that I had been carrying, but I was enjoying it. However, something was missing, and I was not completely satisfied or fully committed to a major in French!

In the summer of 1975, Gwen and I were married, and we returned to California for our second year so that she could finish her nursing program. I registered for more French classes and the school year started. One was an evening class called "The Literature of French Speaking Africa." On the second night I began to seriously question myself about what I was studying, and why. I asked myself, "What am I doing here? I am not a literature guy, and I don't have any interest whatsoever in the literature and poetry of other cultures." At that time I did not yet know how to articulate the question, "What are you pretending not to know?"

When I got home that night, I said to Gwen, "I'm not really enjoying this class, and if I am really honest with myself, my heart is not in this French/Education major either. In my heart what I really want to do is to study to become a pastor and work back home in Canada."

I had not meant to throw her that curve. She had decided at one point that she didn't want to marry a pastor, and now the guy she was married to wanted to become a pastor. What could she say? She supported my decision, and the next day I went in and changed all my classes. I began to seriously study religion and theology. It was the best education decision I could have made. My heart was peaceful, I was alive inside, and I never looked back. In September of 1976, I registered back in Canada for my final year and graduated with a theology degree in May of 1977.

In June of 1977, I began pastoring my first church district, two small congregations in Dartmouth and Truro, Nova Scotia.

Two years later, we attended Theological Seminary in Berrien Springs, Michigan, and I graduated from there with a Master of Divinity Degree in 1982.

We returned from Seminary, and through the years we pastored churches in Prince Edward Island, New Brunswick, British Columbia, and Alberta.

From my childhood on, and through my years of study, I have learned many things about Jesus. I am someone who loves to read, and I have read several books about Jesus before, during, and since my years in school and seminary. I have preached countless sermons about Jesus. I have knowledge about Him and who He is and claims to be. I have attempted to present Him well to people whenever I am given the opportunity to do so.

When I resigned from pastoring in April of 2000 and began this wilderness journey, I realized that I knew a lot *about* Jesus, but I was now going to find out if I really knew Jesus personally. It's a very different thing to know about someone than to personally and intimately know that person. What I needed to know was whether this Jesus I had met and known of for so many years was someone who had time or interest in me after a failure of this magnitude.

As I started on this wilderness journey of sorting out my truth and understanding about life, of all the lessons I had to learn, the most important was, "Does God, does His Son Jesus, really still love someone such as me?" I was fully aware that I had clearly demonstrated the human condition in the choices I had made. The question was, could this Jesus love and save even me? "I know about God, I know the theology and I know the theory. The words are easy on my tongue, but do they resonate with my heart? Are they real to me?"

People encouraged me to trust God and believe His word. That was all sweet and good, and helpful, but in the end, it came down to one thing. "Did I believe what Jesus said? Did I trust God to mean what He said?"

On several occasions in my life, I had crossed paths with a pastor friend who greatly impacted my life. He was a traveling preacher who taught on a variety of topics in various places around the world. I had the privilege of attending his seminars on a few different occasions, and even had him teach his workshops in churches I pastored from time to time.

One day I heard he was going to be in Vancouver on vacation. He lived in the United States, and I had not seen him for several years. I got in touch with him, and he invited me over for a visit, so I hopped a flight to go see him. He was staying in a beautiful, vacation exchange home in the city where he was simply enjoying some rest and relaxation. We sat out on the back deck enjoying a sunny afternoon as I caught him up on the changes in my life. He was gracious as always. His love for Jesus and grace for people was always evident. He did not in any way judge or reject me. In fact, taught me a lesson I will never forget.

He asked me to read a Bible Passage in Romans 5:6-10, and he asked, "Can you tell me, from this passage, what four of the human conditions are named here that Jesus died for?" I read the passage and they were not too hard to find. In verse 6 it says, "For while we were still weak, at the right time Christ died for the ungodly." Then, in verse 8, I read, "God shows His love for us in that while we were still sinners, Christ died for us." I found the last one in verse 10 where it says, "while we were enemies we were reconciled to God by the death of His Son."

I answered him and said, "He died for the weak, the ungodly, the sinners and the enemies."

Then he brought home what he wanted me to see with the question. "Do any of those conditions describe you? If these are the conditions Jesus died for, do you qualify?"

I was deeply moved as I took in what he had just made so obvious. Finally, I spoke. "I have been weak, I have acted ungodly, I have demonstrated that I am a sinner, and as a sinner I am an enemy of God." With a smile on my face and in my heart, I added, "I guess I qualify!" The truth about what God thought of me was becoming real to me in a brand-new way.

But he didn't stop there. He asked, "Were the qualifications past tense or were they current when He died?" I admitted that all of them were in the "while we were still" tense. It was clearly stated that He did not wait for us to stop being those things first, and then change all those things before He decided to die for us. He died for us "while we were still" in any or all of those conditions.

My friend then added that we don't need to stop at the end of the day and ask for forgiveness. We instead need to stop at the end of the day and acknowledge that "I have been weak today and demonstrated that I am a sinner in need of you. Thank you that I am one of the people you have already died for. I qualify!"

I couldn't deny it. It was there in black and white. It was a truth that resonated DEEPLY with my heart and soul. It was the Word of God, and He was personally telling me this to answer my fears. I didn't need to beg for forgiveness in order to receive His mercy and love. It was there in His Word, and it clearly said that He loved and died for me while I was still in that human condition.

I saw Jesus again in a way that I had never seen Him before. I met Him in my childhood, I learned about Him in college, seminary, and in studying about Him for years and decades. I had preached about Him often. And, I loved Him. That day however, was different. I met Jesus again, as if for the very first time. It really connected, deep within me, that I was safe in His love. I had seen it before in other contexts, but in my wilderness journey it was like I was meeting Him all over again. I truly was sorry. He knew that, and I knew that He knew that. But this passage told me He died for me before I was even sorry. He died for me and had everything in place for me so that when I saw Him for who He truly is, the message of His love would come home to me and bring the peace He wanted me to experience.

Maybe you have at some time been struggling and wondering, or even believing, that your life is too broken for God to forgive after "all you've done." I want to encourage you to read that passage in Romans for yourself. If you qualify, as I do, then like me, you are safe in His love.

I easily get emotional at times of meditation on the life of Jesus. His actions among the people He rubbed shoulders with are not just stories to me anymore, they are about me. In the stories where He forgives people's sins, I see myself in their place. I see myself as the one He does not condemn. He sits patiently and listens to me pour my heart out. This is the Jesus I personally and intimately know.

I can tell you about Him, but I can't push Him into your heart. You are the one who must accept Him. He promised, "if you believe in Him, you will not perish but will have eternal life." His sacrifice is in your place. He is the Savior, big enough to get us all off of this planet, to a much better place. That is His goal and His plan, and He will not fall short of that. It is a most gracious offer. A free gift from God Himself. Forgiveness and eternal life in exchange for recognizing that my human condition qualifies me for His love. Amazing!!

I had this personally illustrated in a most profound way. I'm embarrassed to tell you that despite all caution, I one day fell for an internet scam. I should have been, and believed I was much smarter, but I was not. It's a little like Eve. How often she might have said, "I should have known better and just believed what God had said!" The result of her decision was sealed and there was no way to get it back. The result of my failure to think clearly was sealed. I lost money and there would be no way to get it back. I was the loser.

It went like this. I got an email asking for help from a member of the church where I was pastor. I knew her and the email looked valid. I even double checked it with a friend. I wrote back and asked how I could help her. She explained that she was out of town and asked if I could purchase two gift cards that she needed for a friend whom she was helping to prepare a birthday party. She would pay me when she got home. I fell for it. This lady never emails me and that should have been a red flag. I never once thought to check with her family. It was a no brainer to me. I believed it was her, she needed help and I was willing to help.

I followed her instructions and did what she asked. She quickly thanked me but then apologized that she had not known her friend actually needed even more cards. Could I send four more? Well, of course! She needed help and I trusted her. I took care of that too, and she then apologetically asked one more time for four more. When I followed the instructions for the last ones it suddenly hit me! This is fake; this is not her at all. I had just been scammed and foolishly gave away $1,000.00 in Amazon gift cards to someone I didn't even know. I thought I was helping, and instead I got ripped off for a lot of money that I did not have to give.

I called her son to ask if she was out of town, and he practically cried for me. He knew that others had gotten the same email, but he didn't know that I had. She was not traveling and had never left home; someone had hacked her email and I was dealing with a scam-artist who had just ripped me off. Her husband called me later to get the full story and I could hardly tell him what I had done because it was so obvious that I had been very foolish and had not been thinking clearly at all. I was deeply humiliated at my stupidity.

A couple of days later he called me again and asked me to stop by his house, which I did. When I got there, he said, "You were legitimately trying to help my wife. You were doing it because you are a caring man. I so appreciate your willingness to help her, even though it was not her. I want you to have this." He held out his hand and in it was a check for $1,000.00, the exact amount I had lost.

As he stood there holding out that check, my mind quickly realized I had at least three options. I could say "No, I will not take that money. I made the mistake; I will pay for it myself. This had nothing to do with you. I will not allow you to give me anything back."

Also, I could have said, "I will not take all of that, I will split it with you. Thank you, but I will meet you halfway. Please rewrite the check and make it $500."

Or I could reach my hand out to take the check and, with gratitude for the graciousness of this man and with a humble heart, go and cash it and be fully restored, back to where I started. Even though he had nothing to do with it, he would then be the one who bore the cost of my mistake.

This is just like the offer that Jesus makes to us. We are the descendants of people who made the mistake. We live with the human condition we were born with. We demonstrate that condition every day as we go about life. We think and do things that do not always line up with the life and plans God wants for us.

He says, "I love you so much I sent my only begotten Son, that whosoever believes in Him will not perish but have everlasting life."

John 3:16. Jesus left Heaven and took on human flesh forever so He could be with us. Everything changed for Him so that He could rescue you and me. Then He holds out His hand and says, here it is, will you accept My offer?

Not unlike the offer of my friend with his check in his outstretched hand, there are three options.

We can say to God, "No, this is my mistake, I'm the one who sins, you should not have to pay. I won't accept your gift. I'm too ashamed and embarrassed." And He pleads and says "It's already paid, please take it. It was paid while you were still an enemy, and a weak, ungodly sinner."

A second choice would be that we could say, "I'll meet you halfway. I'll shape up my act, I'll be and do better. I can't expect you to pay it all. I'll show you how perfect I can be and earn your gift to me." However, the reality is that it's all His gift. We cannot earn it. We cannot be good enough, and even if we were, we are still carrying the human condition with its bent toward sin.

Or, the third option is, we can say, "Thank You! I have nothing to offer, I'm speechless. You would do this for me? I get to spend eternity with you because of your gift to me? Yes, I will accept your gift. Count me in." That's the answer He's truly hoping all of us will give.

It matters not the nature of the mistakes, or the number of mistakes we have made. It's the written down truth that if we qualify, He's already paid for it.

By the way, in humble gratitude, I reached out, took the man's check and went to cash it. I was financially restored to where I had been, because of a gracious gift by one who had no obligation or reason to pay me back.

I've done the same with Jesus. I have come to truly know Him and that His love and grace is real in spite of how I have lived. I have accepted His offer of free forgiveness and grace. His gift is the guarantee of restoration to the beautiful plan He had for all of us in the beginning. All it takes is admission that we qualify. I hope you take Him at His word and accept it, too.

LESSONS LEARNED

1. Knowing about Jesus is not the same as knowing Jesus!

2. Knowing Jesus intimately is the best friendship and relationship one can ever have.

3. God loves me while I am a sinner and before I am repentant. My weakness demonstrates that I qualify as one for whom Jesus died.

4. Trusting Jesus is the ultimate "Finish Well" scenario. Regardless of past mistakes, He provides the way to find our way back home to Him.

COMPASS POINTS

1. When you look at your life, do you see evidence of the human condition? Explain.

2. What leadership qualities do you think would be necessary to save planet Earth from the myriad of global challenges we face? Who among us is able to provide that leadership?

3. What qualities would be necessary to be able to change the human heart and heal the human condition? Who among us is able to provide that healing?

4. With the list of conditions listed, "Weak, Ungodly, Sinners, Enemies" do you qualify for the gift Jesus wants to give you? How so?

We must step firmly and positively on the ground before us because we do not know what the next day might hold. We may have much time to enjoy life, but we may not, so we need to keep busy living it with intention.

From the Wilderness

She stood in the storm and when the wind did not blow her way, she adjusted her sails.

Elizabeth Edwards

The Bible often says, 'It came to pass.'
It never says, 'It came to stay."

From the Wilderness

28

WHEN DOES THE WILDERNESS JOURNEY END?

While I speak a lot of the challenges of this wilderness journey, I hope you can see that there have been many bright and happy events as well as surprises along the way. These moments were like a desert "oasis" that filled the journey with anticipation and hope for things I had yet to experience. I did not know what was ahead, and I did not know when I would be able to say I was done with the wilderness.

Moses had defining events that made it clear when he entered and when he left his wilderness journey. Forty years after he left Egypt amid fear and scandal, God spoke to him directly out of a burning bush, and informed him that He had a work to do in order to deliver His people who were still back in Egypt. It was time to leave. While hesitant, and even resistant, he went, and the continuing story of Moses is referenced in different ways throughout the entire Bible.

I have not yet had any such defining moment, as Moses did, to mark the end of my journey. I might conclude that when I was invited to pastor again in 2014, that this marked the end of the journey. Maybe it was when I retired from pastoring with dignity in 2020. Maybe God still has a calling on my life that I have not yet discovered. Maybe there is a burning bush yet in my future where God will clearly lay out a plan for me. It could be that there are always lessons to learn and that, in a sense, there is always a wilderness element to life. Life is often not an easy road, for any of us.

Even with my life so full and satisfying in many ways at this time, there are times that make it clear that life is not free from dry or hard events.

Gwen and I were blessed with the privilege of raising two daughters. Kristen was born in Halifax, Nova Scotia while we pastored the Seventh-day Adventist church across the harbor in Dartmouth. Karin was born right on schedule during Christmas break in Toronto, Ontario, during the time we were attending seminary in Michigan.

We had all the joys and challenges of parenting, like any family. Our girls lived the nomad life of a pastor's family with grace. I am sure there were feelings of upheaval that challenged these young girls as we moved about, forcing them to change schools and friends on a semi-regular basis.

Kristen and Karin went to college at Walla Walla College, in the state of Washington. Karin graduated in 2003 with a degree in Graphic Design. She has an incredible talent for seeing beauty and creativity in the world around her and can make it come alive in numerous ways. I love to brag about her, and her work.

Kristen graduated from the nursing program in 2004. After two years of nursing work with cancer children in Loma Linda, California, she moved to Seattle to work in the Seattle Children's Hospital. She is my daughter, and I will shamelessly brag about her too. She made an incredible impact on the children and families she was able to minister to through her nursing. The stories I have heard of the difference she has made in the lives of others makes me extremely proud of her.

In August of 2018, it was discovered that she had a serious form of cancer that had already begun to spread within her body. Of course, we were not ready to hear that news. No family ever is, and the news landed hard on all of us. We were in shock, not able to properly process the unfolding information. The details we learned in the next twenty-four hours were a blur as more tests were done, and information was clarified. The news was not good at any level. We all realized that Kristen was into the fight of her life, and we rallied around to support her. The many questions we had regarding treatment protocol were answered in the following days, and Kristen bravely entered a wilderness of her own.

As she was initially talking with our family about what had just been discovered in the test just an hour earlier that morning, my mind was interrupted. The thought that came to me was clear enough to be a voice, but I'm not sure that it actually was. The message was, "You have been praying for this girl. Trust Me, I've got this." I had no doubt it was a direct message from God to me and our family.

I did not know for sure what it meant; I only knew what the message was. I didn't know if it meant she would be healed, or if it was a message to tell me that no matter what happened, God was present to walk the road with her and with us. I do know that the peace that came over me at that moment never left me. I often referred back to that moment and reminded God that He had promised me that He "had this" in His control. I was good with that.

This event took place after eighteen years into my wilderness journey. I had learned many things about God, and I was confident of His presence in my life and in the life of my family. I knew that He was close, and I conveyed to everyone that God had promised His presence even at this dark time.

Many significant events took place, but two things stand out strongly in my memory from those early days.

The next day, when she got her test results and knew the reality of what she was dealing with, she talked openly about what it all might mean and the full reality of what she was facing. She was fully aware that this story may not have a good ending. Then, after the conversation slowed down a bit, she confidently stated, "Well, I'm not dying today and I'm not going to die tomorrow, so let's get on with living. We're going to beat this." That's a good reminder for all of us to step firmly and positively on the ground before us because we do not know what the next day might hold. We may have much time to enjoy life, but we may not, so we need to keep busy living it with intention.

Our family was all together that day, as she shared the information. We tossed around all the "what now" scenarios and realized that we had much to learn yet about what the next steps would be. Kristen kind of wrapped up the time by saying, "I need you all on my side. I can't take care of you or look after your emotions. I will have too much to do to look after myself and I need you to take care of yourselves. Let's be a strong family and a "together" family as we move forward."

It's so true that we serve each other well when we make the effort to take care of ourselves so that we are not taking emotional strength from another, especially when they need every ounce they can find. We needed to give everything we could to support her and not require anything from her.

A second strong memory came three weeks later. I was back in Seattle to be with her as she received her very first chemo treatment.

How does a young woman face those events with grace and strength? How does a dad watch that strong chemical be pumped into his firstborn daughter's body without fear and concern? We were in a brand-new wilderness place as a family.

I stayed the night with her to make sure she was okay, and then had to take the bus and train to the airport to fly home. She rode the bus into downtown Seattle with me, and we got off to have lunch at one of her favorite restaurants before we went our separate ways.

I will always remember that we sat at a window table at the Café Yumm! and watched people go by on the street as we chatted. She talked openly about the journey ahead. She was strong, courageous, and determined. She was going to give this fight everything she had. As we talked, she said, "I have no time to judge or criticize any person because I don't know what they are dealing with. I don't know what has brought them to this moment. I want to have grace for everyone." Then, looking out the window at a lady struggling to walk due to her physical condition, she said, as she motioned toward her, "I have no right to judge that lady. I have no idea what has happened in her life to make her the way she is. I just want to love everyone."

What a powerful example of a great way to live. How peaceful we become inside when we remove criticism, blame and condemnation from our thoughts and vocabulary. And, what a gift to the people around us if we look for the good in them and be gracious with their lives. She was my teacher that day.

Kristen fought a good fight. She changed everything she needed to in her diet and was determined to live a very healthy lifestyle. She walked, laughed, and worked hard to make memories. She believed that God could bless her and heal her. She also knew that He was close, and He had promised, "I've got this." Kristen was also realistic and knew that this cancer journey may not have a good ending.

Five months after her diagnosis, at Christmas of 2018, she asked that we not spend money on each other. Instead, she wanted to create memories with the things we did and the money we spent. She asked for and arranged to have a family photo shoot. She wanted nothing more than to live a long life, but she was preparing for a different outcome if required.

Kristen lost her battle to that cancer on September 18, 2019. Five days earlier she told Karin that, "I think I can still turn this around." She was optimistic in every fiber of her body. Thanks to care and good medication, she passed away peacefully as we along with close friends who loved her deeply stood by her side. And I remembered the words I heard that first morning, "I've got this!"

I don't know yet what that statement fully means, but I trust it completely. I have a belief that one day we will get to have a one-on-one with God, and we will get to ask any question we want, knowing that we will get a full and complete answer. There will be complete transparency. I want to ask God to show me what, "I've got this!" meant through His eyes. I want to see her story through His eyes, and what He was watching and doing. I'm not angry at Him, not even for a moment. I know that He knows things I don't know, and I also know that we live in a broken world. People die who should be alive, living out their purpose and full potential. He is not the God of death; He is the God of life. I have a strong faith that one day our family will be together again, and that thought keeps me with my nose pressed against the window, watching as I anticipate His return to make His promises all real.

In the meantime, I think about how my emotions are sometimes packed up and tight, like the boxes under the stairs. I think about things we did and said to each other. I sometimes think of things we might have said to each other. We have many great family memories, before and after she got sick. I think about the memories created as she lived large in her world. The greatest thing about Kristen was that I didn't realize her impact on the world until after she was gone. I say it's the greatest thing because this tells me she lived out her life purpose, but didn't make a big deal or brag about it. She just silently went about doing what she did best; loving kids, families and others who needed love.

I read stories and memories that people wrote. I visited with people and received phone calls from strangers who just wanted to tell me how she had impacted their children as she did her best to take care of their needs and calm their fears. She didn't flaunt her loving ways or tell me all the good she was doing. She just quietly lived her life of love and generosity for the good of others.

She had watched children die of cancer, and now she faced it herself. I never heard her complain or pound her fist and ask, "Why me?" She may have done that at times when she was alone, and I could not blame her if she did. But what I did see was a strong heart, determined to give life her all, and then peacefully submit to the path that had her name on it. She makes me proud beyond words as I write this.

I recently saw a Facebook quote that I think describes her well. It reads, "I love people that have no idea how wonderful they are and just wander around making the world a better place."

Elizabeth Edwards could have been writing about Kristen, perfectly when she said, "She stood in the storm and when the wind did not blow her way, she adjusted her sails."

What this part of the journey taught me, is that even while in many ways my wilderness has improved, and is maybe even behind me, there are some very dry spots in life even yet. No parent wants to say good-by to a child, but we are not the first. We follow a great crowd of parents who have had to do it before us, and we also know that others will join us as time moves on.

We were a normal family that experienced our seasons of tension and questions, but those memories don't matter anymore. Like the boxes under the stairs, it's just as well that those stay packed away and then are just thrown away. But, I cannot ignore the sweet memories and emotions of the forty years we had with Kristen, and leave them packed up. I want those emotions and my sadness for her to be real on my tongue. It's much more wonderful to laugh about her today, and sometimes shed a few tears, as we stand by her grave and remember times and moments that should never be forgotten.

I have learned through this experience that, even in the wilderness, there can be extra dry and lonely places. I don't expect life on planet Earth to be easy. There are paths ahead that if we knew what was coming, we might just stop and give up. However, we don't have to live each day in fear of that. I believe the Bible clearly spells out how the story ends and it's going to be amazing when we get there. We can instead live today to the fullest. We can create memories, even with or without a cancer diagnosis hanging over our heads. We can make sure that we laugh and tell each other that we love them. Enjoy the gift of life and love and express it. It can make the driest desert come to life.

When Kristen had friends visit her toward the end, she never wanted to say good-bye because she didn't want it to sound final. So, she would just say, "See you next time!" From my reading of the Bible, I believe that she rests in sleep, waiting for Jesus to keep His promise that He will come again and get rid of death forever. When that happens, He will wake her up and we will see her again. She will again be beautiful, healthy and strong. Able to live forever. My worldview includes the firm belief that our "next time" is not far away, and ALL wilderness journeys, for everyone, will end.

LESSONS LEARNED

1. Even in the darkest hours God has not left us. In fact, He is very present, and no doubt wants us to know that "He's got this!"

2. Wilderness journeys may have extra lessons to be learned, but it's all for a greater purpose.

3. We don't have to wait for bad news to live an on-purpose life. We can intentionally live on purpose and make a difference, beginning right now!

COMPASS POINTS

1. Where do you find strength when you face hard days, and yet another wilderness?

ABOUT ME

Gwen and I have been married since 1975, and we live in Red Deer, Alberta, Canada. We have had the privilege of parenting two beautiful daughters, Kristen and Karin.

Kristen passed away on September 18, 2019, from an aggressive cancer.

Karin is married to Enoch Ross and there is nothing better than spending time with them along with our sweet and precious grandchildren, Elsa and Henry.

I graduated in 1977 with a BTh (Bachelor of Theology) and again in 1982 with a MDiv (Master of Divinity). It has been a great life journey to be the pastor of churches in Nova Scotia, Prince Edward Island, New Brunswick, British Columbia and Alberta. It has also been rewarding to have studied and been certified as a Mediator and Professional Life Coach.

I am truly living on purpose whenever given the opportunity to meet and help people discover all the richness of life possible here on planet Earth, but am even more passionate about encouraging people to prepare for an eternal life beyond this one. To end up there is the ultimate reality of Finishing Well.

It is easy for me to look for the bright side of life and seek out any experience that includes fun, enjoyment, and laughter. Golf is a challenging hobby that brings friendship and exercise into my life, and much of my laughter comes from some of the poor shots I have made. Reading is also a never-ending source of pleasure for me, and through the years I have collected an extensive library of books on many topics. Although I'm not always successful, the challenge of finishing a book a week is something that pushes me each year.

However, more important than anything already mentioned, I am committed to pursuing a personal relationship with God and Jesus Christ. The journey is awkward and messy at times as life's lessons are learned, but it is the foundation in my life that brings me peace and contentment. The ongoing adventure of it all gets me up in the morning with anticipation for what the day holds

ACKNOWLEDGEMENTS

Whoever thought I would write a book!? Not me!

I could never have done it alone. I have discovered how many are involved to bring a project like this to completion. I received encouragement, feedback, and support from so many friends, for which I am grateful.

Gwen was very patient and understanding of the untold hours I spent in front of my keyboard. While my story also exposes parts of her story, she supported me every step of the journey. She is the wind beneath my wings.

I have many people to thank for my journey and the lessons you taught me along the way. I wish I could name all of you, but since I cannot, I didn't even start. I knew I would miss someone. You all are a gift in my life and have helped to define my journey. Many of you will recognize yourself in these pages. To those of you who do not know how you have impacted me, you are no less important.

I want to thank my daughter Karin for the awesome book cover and helpful insight into how to make the book look great. Her creative eye and graphic design skills never cease to impress me.

The cover picture is courtesy of my cousin, Frank Spangler, who personally took this photograph in the desert area that could very possibly be a place where Moses walked during his wilderness journey.

I am extremely grateful to my life coach friend Gene Hartmann who invested hours into reading the manuscript and helping me find the right words for the Compass Points. He is a master at asking good questions and I am indebted to his work and input on how to do it better than I could have ever done it on my own.

Finally, I am not exaggerating in the least when I say that this book would not be what it is without the help of Heather Russell. It started with a simple statement several years ago when I said to her, "I want to write a book, I just don't know how to begin. I would for sure need an editor." She responded, "I'm an editor!" That was the beginning, and here it is! I worked at it in stages, sometimes putting it on the shelf for a period of years, but always with the intention of seeing it through to the end. Each time I would contact Heather, she was faithfully available to help whenever I was ready to pick it back up again. Staying at home during the Covid pandemic provided the catalyst for the final space of time to do what it took to complete the project. You hold in your hands the end result of the countless hours she worked to check my grammar and make sure that my words would fit together well and make logical sense. She has my deep and heartfelt gratitude.

Feel free to check out more at Finishwell.ca

You are welcome to contact me at bill@finishwell.ca

Manufactured by Amazon.ca
Bolton, ON

26133947R00153